The Internet is the biggest ion and learning since the advent o̶ ̶ ̶ ̶ ̶ ̶ ̶ ̶ ̶ ars ago. It will destroy the traditiona̶ ̶ ̶ ̶ ̶ ̶ ̶ ̶ ̶ . an even better way to learn, and to ̶ ̶ ̶ ̶ ̶ ̶ . Almost every teacher, from professional trainers to college professors to Sunday School teachers, will learn a different way of teaching.

Learners will learn more, while working at their own speed, time and manner, over the Internet. The average class will have 1,000 participants; anyone can ask a question and get an individual and personal response from the instructor. A daily test or quiz will tell you exactly what you have mastered and what areas you still need to work on. Learners will come from all over the world, and they will form a virtual community that will kindle long-term relationships.

Online learning will constitute 50% of all learning in the 21st century. It will create tremendous opportunities for teachers, trainers, business owners, educators, consultants, associations, volunteer and part time teachers. The Internet will do for our society what the automobile did for it in the last century. And lifelong learning is the engine that will drive our information age economy.

In this book William A. Draves, the foremost authority on lifelong learning, shows you how to develop and teach your online course. With information you won't find anywhere else, he will help you position your expertise and your course for long-term success.

After reading *Teaching Online*, you will have the latest and most advanced information about conducting an educational program, course, seminar, conference, customer education, meeting or training online. You will know how the Internet will change how we learn, how to plan your online course, how to develop content, interaction and assessment, how to teach online, and much more.

Welcome to the 21st century. Welcome to online learning.

Teaching Online

William A. Draves

Published by LERN Books, a division of the Learning Resources Network (LERN), P.O. Box 9, River Falls, Wisconsin 54022, U.S.A.

Library of Congress Catalog Card Number: 99-65463
Draves, William A., 1949-
    Teaching Online

ISBN 1-57722-016-1

Printing
7 6 5 4 3 2 1

Dedication

Several years ago I discovered that my oldest son, Jason, was more computer literate than I would ever be. I began asking him questions, and then asking his friends questions. I looked over his shoulder at his chat room, watched him develop a part-time business on the Web, and saw him do his homework using the resources of the Web. Jason has been on the cutting edge of life in the Information Age, and I have learned much from him.

When Sammie Jackson came to live with us, I was bent on mentoring him through high school. But in a few short months it became apparent that I would learn more from him than I could teach him. Sammie understood another culture, another way of thinking, another value system. He also believed that race and culture should make no difference; he judged no one by their color, and he asked the same in return. Sammie has been on the cutting edge of culture in the Information Age, and I have learned much from him.

When Willie was just two years old, I took him, his crayons and paper with me while shopping. The store keeper looked at Willie's drawing and told him he would be an artist some day. Willie looked up and firmly replied, "I am an artist." A child of the 21st century, Willie can envision space travel while I cannot. He can think about life a million years ago, or hence. He can also draw, make up jokes, and write a great fictional story. Willie is on the cutting edge of art and relationships in the Information Age, and I have learned much from him.

I dedicate this book to my three sons, Jason Coates, Sammie Jackson and Willie Draves, representatives of the online generation who have taught me much about the 21st century.

Cover Artwork

The artwork on the cover of the book is done by Gina Capaldi of San Dimas, California. It first appeared on the brochure cover of the Los Angeles Harbor College Extension Program in Wilmington, Calif., Carla Mussa-Muldoon, director. Both the artist and the continuing education program have a knack for hitting on important themes in our culture. For this author, the drawing of the Scarecrow on the Internet connected the transition of the last century, as represented by the L.Frank Baum book *The Wizard of Oz*, with the current transition to the Information Age and learning online.

Acknowledgments

Many people influenced my thinking and taught me about the Internet. A few them include training and learning guru and Vice President for the American Society of Training and Development, Ed Schroer; master web developer Cem Erdem; New York University administrator Dorothy Durkin; Empire State University administrator and past Chair of the LERN Board Hugh Hammett; and e-mail guru Lenny Charnoff. Special thanks to my brother, Timothy Draves of San Antonio, for the 1909 brochure, which led to my research on Frankfort, Kansas.

Many people also assisted me in producing this book. They include LERN's Assistant to the President Julia Quick; desktop and layout artist extraordinaire Danita Dickinson Ahrens; desktopper Sandy Davis; copy editor Glenna Wilson; and my colleague and companion Julie Coates Draves.

TABLE OF CONTENTS

Introduction
Welcome to Teaching Online

In the 21ˢᵗ century, half of all learning will be conducted on the Internet. The opportunities are tremendous for teaching online.

The biggest market for learning online will be adults. Adults at work will need to be involved in learning for up to one hour a day. Adults at home will want to learn an increasingly diverse number of subjects, from the inner workings of the brain to how to live in outer space.

Here are just some of the opportunities for teaching online:

- Training for business and industry, especially by occupation and specialties, such as vacuum repair or time management for secretaries.
- Customer education, as every business will want to provide education and training for its customers on how to use its products and keep up with the industry.
- Personal interest courses, from stamp collecting to growing mango trees.
- Social service and civic education, from health and wellness to increasing local voter turnout in your community.
- Continuing professional education, in every occupational specialty.
- College credit and degree programs, in increasingly diverse subject areas.
- Elementary and secondary education, helping children in school in math, science and more, from remedial to gifted levels.

If you have an area of expertise, you can teach online. Those teaching online will include business owners, consultants, trainers, college professors, school teachers, social service workers, authors, writers, experts and speakers. You need only two things to teach online: an area of expertise and a prospective audience.

In this book, we will show you how to tap into the enormous opportunity of teaching online. We will help you become the best instructor for your particular subject area, the first in your niche topic area to go online, and then assist you in having the largest online class in your topic area.

But there will also be many people who fail at teaching online. They will fail primarily not because they are poor teachers, but because they did not design their online course to meet the requirements for success in the new environment of the Information Age. The purpose of this book is not to help you teach online, but to help you teach online successfully. At the end of this book, you will understand how to structure your course, how to prepare for it, how to teach it and how to promote it. You will know how to succeed in teaching online. Welcome to the era of lifelong learning. Welcome to the era of learning online.

Part I.
Learning in the
21st Century

Chapter 1
Lifelong Learning
in the 21st Century

For more than 20 years, I lived in Manhattan, Kansas. But I did not grow up in Kansas. I grew up in Wisconsin. Kansas has mandatory continuing education. And so whenever someone moves to Kansas, in order to gain residency, they have to take a class on the *Wizard of Oz*. So I signed up for my class on the *Wizard of Oz*, the most famous American fairy tale ever written.

It turns out that the *Wizard of Oz* was written a little over 100 years ago, in 1896. The movie came out in the 1930s. But L. Frank Baum wrote the book at the turn of the last century. *The Wizard of Oz* is about the transition society was going through at that time. Up until that time we were an agrarian society. Most people earned their living by farming. Baum saw that things were going to be different, that we were going to move into what would become known as the Industrial Age. He knew that life would be totally different. He understood somehow that the attitudes and the values of the agrarian pastoral society, which people had known, and he had known, and was what made America wonderful and great — that all of that was going to change. And he was against that. He thought that was awful. And so he created the scarecrow and the tin man and the lion to represent the virtues of the agrarian society. And he set it in Kansas because Kansas was like California in the 1860s. It was the land of golden opportunity. He had never been to Kansas. But 10 years before he wrote the book, a New York newspaper man named Horace Greeley said, "Go west, young man." And back then people actually believed New York journalists. And so a million and a half people moved to Kansas within about 10 years. It was a huge migration. Back then

3

Kansas was a symbol of prosperity and the good life. And that's why he set it in Kansas because he was saying, "Even in Kansas, this awful transition is happening."

Baum was right, of course. Everything did change. The Industrial Age took people off the family farm and moved them into cities. And it changed not only our way of life, but our values and attitudes. Your great grandparents lived very differently. Today we don't grow up in extended families. We don't spend weeks every year canning fruits and vegetables for the winter. We don't get our fresh vegetables from the garden. We don't rest on Sundays. Kids don't help with the chores at an early age. Most of us don't hunt. We no longer view a handshake as binding.

And now 100 years later we are going through another gut-wrenching total change in society. It's not just the turning of the century that we are witness to. It's not just the changing of the millennium. But it is the moving from one age, the Industrial Age that all of us adults have grown up in and know, into the next age — the Information Age.

And so I don't think it is a coincidence that Los Angeles Harbor College, a lifelong learning program that often captures the spirit of what America is thinking about, recently had a brochure cover showing the scarecrow from the *Wizard of Oz* now on the Internet.

Throughout the 10,000-year history of humankind, no one taught on the Internet. Teaching online is a totally new experience. And it is taking place as part of a totally transforming economic, social and personal change in the way we live, work, think and believe. I tell you the story of the *Wizard of Oz* because it relates very much to what you and I are going through today, transitioning from one world into another more unknown world. And because one of the best ways to understand what is happening to us is to look at the people and times when it happened before.

Teaching online will not be the same as teaching in-person. It will not mean simply being able to use a new technology, like a slide projector or fax machine.

In order to be able to understand how to teach online, we need to talk about lifelong learning in the 21st century, and how it will be totally different from learning in the 20th century.

The year 1991 was the first year of the Information Age. In that year business for the first time spent more money on software and computers than they did on equipment and capital expenditures.

Before 1991, business wasn't all that hot on training its employees. Training was regarded as a cost. If a company had a little bit of money left over, it might send its employees to a seminar. But the typical boss worried that if employees were trained, they might leave the company. And that's how the average employer thought. After 1991, more employers started to think of training as an investment rather than a cost. And so employers don't worry as much now what happens if they train their employees and they leave. Today they worry about what happens if they don't train their people and they stay. And that is a much worse nightmare than the other scenario.

The American public is ahead of employers in their outlook on the importance of learning, education and training. In 1995, for example, the first in-depth study on adult learning appeared since Allen Tough's *The Adult's Learning Projects* in 1971. Washington State University's Don Dilman did a national study asking the question, "Is additional training or education important for you to be successful in your work?" It turns out that 80 percent of Americans said yes. It's important — not nice, not desirable, but important. This figure is much higher than any of us in adult education or continuing education could ever have hoped for.

The other interesting thing about this study is that the importance of education and training cuts across all segments of the population. If you analyze it by educational level, it is basically 80 percent. You do it by age, and yes, younger people value education a little bit more than people who are working at age 60. But basically the support level remains at 80 percent. And poor people who earn less than $20,000 a year value education as highly or even more highly than those who make $60,000 or more. And so the majority of Americans understand that learning is now important for their work.

In the early 1970s, they understood that lifelong learning was great, fun and wonderful, and thousands of personal development classes were offered, and are still offered. But now on the work side, Americans are understanding that continuing education and training is important to them.

So lifelong learning is the engine that is driving the Information Age economy.

In lifelong learning, we are at where the automobile was in 1920. If we went back to 1920 and said, "Sir, do you have an automobile?" The respondent would say, "You bet." "Have you driven it recently?" "Of course — ma, didn't we just take the automobile out last Sunday? You bet. We drive that automobile all the time."

Today if you ask somebody if she or he is involved in lifelong learning, continuing education or training, the person will say yes. But if you told that person in 1920 that in 50 years people would be spending one to two hours a day driving their automobiles, what would that person say?

He would say, "Who's going to milk the cows? Who's going to do the chores? You're driving up and down on these gravel roads two hours a day?" And so when I tell people today that in 30 years people will be spending one to two hours a day learning, they do not believe it. They don't see how people will have the time to go to seminars or conferences or classes two hours a day.

But that's exactly what will happen. Because business and our work depend on continued learning, everyone in society will be learning an hour a day. To be able to do that, people will spend half of their learning time online. Online learning will constitute 50 percent of the way people learn. It will not be 100 percent, and we will still have in-person learning, but even in-person learning will be very different from how it is today. The Internet is changing the way we learn.

Chapter 2
How the Internet Will Change How We Learn

The Internet is the biggest technological change in education and learning since the advent of the printed book some 500 years ago. It will destroy the traditional classroom and replace it with an even better way to learn and teach. And almost every learning situation will be totally altered, including training for business and industry, customer education, association conferences and meetings, continuing education, Sunday School classes, leisure learning, college degree programs, even elementary and secondary school education.

Learners will learn more, while working at their own speed, time and manner, over the Internet. The average online class will have from 100 to 1,000 participants; there will be more interaction among teachers and learners than traditional in person presentations; daily quizzes will tell you exactly what you have mastered and what areas you still need to work on. Learners and teachers will come from all over the world, and they will form a virtual community that will kindle long-term relationships.

In the 21st century, online learning will constitute 50 percent of all learning and education. The rapid rise of learning on the Internet will occur not because it is more convenient, cheaper or faster, but because cognitive learning on the Internet is better than learning in-person. Of the growing number of experts seeing this development, Gerald Celente, author of the popular book *Trends 2000*, summarizes it most succinctly: "Interactive, online learning will revolutionize education. The education revolution will have as profound and as far-reaching an effect upon the world as the invention of printing. Not only will it affect where we learn; it also will influence how we learn and what we learn." Recent research reported in the *Washington Post* cites studies showing that online learning is equally as effective as learning in-person. And note that we state "cognitive learning," not all learning.

It is still very early in the development of online learning. But the outlines of the potential of online learning are already emerging. The best guide to the next century lies in history, and in examples of technological transition from the 19th to the 20th century. The automobile and tractor were the driving forces for the Industrial Age. The tractor eventually was demonstrated to not only cover more acres than a horse drawn plow, but to plow deeper (read: better) and thus increase productivity.

Some sectors of society clung to the horse-drawn vehicle, of course. The military still had a cavalry in 1939 to confront Hitler's tanks before the obvious mismatch was addressed. The tractor changed education for the 20th century as well. Prior to the tractor and automobile, one-room schoolhouses were placed every six miles so that a child would have to walk at most three miles to school. The one-room schoolhouse necessitated one teacher and multiple grade levels in one room. With the automobile, people moved into towns, and even rural residents could take buses to school, thus causing school consolidation and the eventual all-but-extinction of the one-room schoolhouse. In the State of Washington, for example, between 1935 and 1939 almost 20 percent of rural one-room schoolhouses were closed.

And when online learning is combined with a more interactive and facilitative in-person learning, it will easily out perform today's outmoded one-size-fits-all traditional lecture delivery system. "Digital media and Internet communications will transform learning practices," notes Peter J. Denning of George Mason University in his *How We Will Learn*.

Here are a few of the effects of online learning that will occur in just a few years:

- The average class size for an online course will be 1,000 participants; already today you can get more than 100 people for an online course.
- The average cost of an online course will plummet to below $100 a course; already today prices of online courses are falling.
- There will be hundreds of thousands of topics from which learners can choose; already today you can learn some things online that you can't find in-person.

But perhaps the most devastating and revolutionary change will be how the Internet will change how we learn. Because as we enter the Information Age, the era of lifelong learning, the era of online learning,

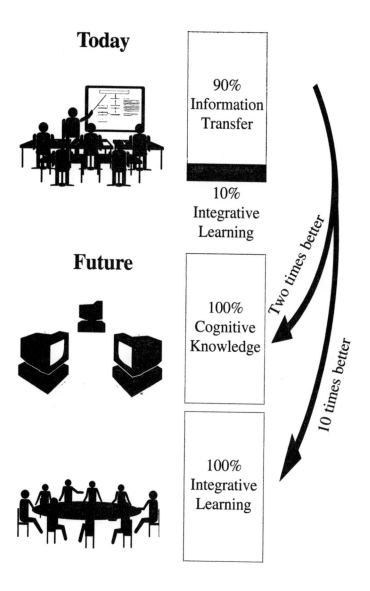

The Internet will break apart the traditional lecture or presentation style of teaching and learning. Two new formats are emerging: online learning, and a different in-person style of learning and teaching.

distance has nothing to do with "distance education." By this I mean that even when the teacher is in close proximity to the learners, the quality of the cognitive learning and teaching will be higher when the cognitive part of the learning is conducted over the Internet. Keoko University in Japan, for example, is already establishing online learning for its on-campus students.

In this chapter I will outline what we already know and can forecast about how the Internet and online learning will change how we learn. We know, for example, that the economic force driving life in the 21st century will be the microchip and the Internet, just as the automobile was the economic force for change in the 20th century. And we know that business will need its workers to learn more, more quickly, and at a lower cost, to remain competitive. We will show that these market forces will create the need and desirability for online learning.

How We Learn Today

For most of history the standard educational setting has been an instructor (or teacher, leader, presenter or speaker) standing in front of a group of people. This is the most common learning design in society, whether it be for college credit classes, noncredit courses, training in business and industry, high school instruction, or even a Sunday School class.

Basically, 90 percent of all education has been "information transfer," the process of transferring information from the teacher's head into the heads of the learners. To do that, teachers have had to talk most of the time. And right up until today that mode of delivery has been the most effective, most efficient, most desirable way to learn.

But as educators we know that the traditional lecture is not the only way to learn. We as learners learn in many different ways, at different times, and from a variety of sources. We also know that learning is not purely a cognitive process, but that it also involves the emotions and even the spirit.

The Internet is destroying the traditional educational delivery system of an instructor speaking, lecturing or teaching in front of one or more learners.

The whole discipline of self-directed learning, variously called adult learning or adult education, has shown that the traditional delivery system is only one way to learn. The Internet represents the biggest technological aid helping people to learn in 500 years, according to many educators.

What the Internet is doing is to explode the traditional method of teaching into two parts — cognitive learning, which can be accomplished better with online learning; and affective learning, which can be accomplished better in a small group discussion setting.

Why Cognitive Learning Can Be Done Better on the Internet

Cognitive learning includes facts, data, knowledge, mental skills — what you can test. And information transfer and cognitive learning can be achieved faster, cheaper and better online.

There are several ways that online learning can be better than classroom learning, such as:

- A learner can learn during her or his peak learning time. My peak learning time is from 10 a.m. to noon. My stepson's peak learning time is between midnight and 3 a.m. He recently signed up for an Internet course and is looking for a couple more, because as he put it, "I have a lot of free time between midnight and 3 a.m." With traditional in-person classes, only some learners will be involved during their peak learning time. The rest will not fully benefit.
- A learner can learn at her or his own speed. With traditional classes, a learner has one chance to hear a concept, technique or piece of knowledge. With online learning, a learner can replay a portion of audio, reread a unit, review a video and retest him or herself.
- A learner can focus on specific content areas. With traditional classes, each content area is covered and given the relative amount of emphasis and time that the teacher deems appropriate. But in a 10-unit course, a given learner will not need to focus on each unit equally. For each of us, there will be some units we know already and some where we have little knowledge. With online learning, we as learners can focus more time, attention and energy on those units, modules or sections of the course where we need the most help and learning.
- A learner can test himself daily. With online learning, a learner can take quizzes and tests easily, instantly receiving the results and finding out how well she or he is doing in a course.
- A learner can interact more with the teacher. Contrary to common opinion today, online learning is more personal and more interactive than traditional classroom courses. In an online course, the instructor has to create the information transfer part of the course — lectures, graphics, text, video — only once. Once the course

units or modules have been developed, there is need only for revisions later on. The instructor is then free to interact with participants in the course.

Learners will acquire the data and facts faster using the Internet. Officials at University Online Publishing, which has been involved in online learning more than most organizations, say that a typical 16-week college course, for example, can be cut to eight weeks because students learn more quickly online.

Finally, technology has consistently driven down costs. Recent reports indicate that education costs grew at over 5 percent for 1998, well above the 3 percent average for all other sectors of the economy. With education costs in the traditional system soaring, technological innovations promise the ability to deliver an education more cheaply.

Downward pressure is already being exerted on prices by online courses. Officials at Regents College in Albany, NY, which collects data on 8,000 distance learning courses, say that prices are dropping already. One community college in Arizona, for example, offers online courses at just $32/credit hour for in-state residents and $67/credit hour for out-of-state learners.

More Interaction Occurs with Online Learning

The heart and soul of an online course will not be the lecture, the delivery, the audio or video. Rather, it will be the interaction between the participants and teacher, as well as the interaction among the participants themselves. This daily interaction among participants, for example, will form what John Hagel, author of *Net Gain*, calls a "virtual community."

The next time you are in a class, count the number of questions asked of the teacher during a one-hour time period. Because of the instructor's need to convey information, the time able to be devoted to questions is very short. In an online course, everyone can ask questions — as many questions as each learner wants or needs.

In an online course, there is also more discussion. If there is a group discussion with 30 people and six to eight people make comments, that is a successful discussion that will take up almost a whole hour. And almost everyone in the group will agree it was lively. Now if you go into an asynchronous discussion forum on the Internet, and 30 people are there, and six to eight are making comments, you will conclude that the discussion is lagging.

The same number of comments on the Internet do not appear to be as lively a discussion as when delivered in person because the capability and capacity of the Internet is that every person can make comments — at the same time. A transcript of a typical online discussion would take hours to give verbally. Online, we can participate in discussions easily, absorbing more information in a much shorter time and engaging in more interaction, not less.

There will be an average of 1,000 learners in a course. This will occur for a number of reasons:

1. There are one thousand people in the world who want to learn any given topic at any given time, even mango trees or Adlai Stevenson.
2. Because people will want to learn from the foremost authority, there will be only two or three online courses for each topic.
3. The cost of an online course will be extremely low, probably under $100, even for credit classes. This will occur because educational institutions can make more money on high volume and low prices than they can on low volume and high prices. It will occur also because the only way an educational institution can lose its market-share for a given course is because the course is priced higher than an alternative course.

Top 10 Reasons

To review, here are my top 10 reasons why cognitive learning on the Internet is BETTER than traditional in-person presentations:

Number 10. You can learn at your own peak learning time of day.

Number 9. You can learn at your own speed.

Number 8. You can learn faster.

Number 7. You can interact more with the teacher.

Number 6. There is more discussion online.

Number 5. Participants come from around the world.

Number 4. You can learn from the foremost authorities and experts.

Number 3. Online learning is less expensive and thus more accessible.

Number 2. Internet links provide more resources.

Number 1. You can form a virtual community.

The Forces Driving Online Learning

There are several forces that will turn this scenario for online learning into reality, and turn it into reality very quickly. They include:

- **Business.** Business will be the biggest force. Business now understands that in order to remain competitive and profitable, it will need employees who are learning constantly. The only cost effective way for this to happen is with online learning.

  So business will require its people to learn online, and it will look to recruit college graduates who can learn online. Colleges and universities will quickly adopt online learning because business will demand that capability from their graduates.

- **Youth.** My children have never taken a computer course. And they never will. Because they are not just computer literate, they grew up in a digital culture. Young people want to learn online. They understand the future, because it is the world in which they must work and compete. Young students will choose online learning.

- **Competition.** Just one provider offering online courses at a low cost and recruiting high volume will force other educational institutions to do the same. In fact, many providers are involved in online learning, and the cost of courses is declining steadily, according to an official at Regents College, which keeps a database of more than 8,000 distance learning courses.

The Impact of Online Learning

Online learning is rapidly becoming recognized as a valid learning delivery system. The number of part-time students in higher education, to name just one educational system, now outnumbers full-time students. The number of colleges offering online courses last year soared to more than 1,000, and the number is growing. Online graduate programs and certificate programs have doubled over one year ago. Online learning has grown exponentially in the business sector, according to Elliot Masie of Saratoga Springs, NY, one of the foremost experts on online training in the workforce. Surveys by the American Society for Training and Development (ASTD) see online training replacing much of on-site training in the near future.

Online learning will do for society what the tractor did for food. A century ago, food was expensive, in limited supply and with very little variety. Today food is relatively cheap, in great supply in our society and with tremendous variety. The Internet will do the same for education.

More people will be able to learn more, for much less cost and with a tremendous variety in choice of topics and subjects. It is something that societies of the past could only dream about. And it will come true for us in a very short time.

An Illustration

In Manhattan, Kansas (alias "the Little Apple"), a college town of 50,000 nestled in the beautiful Flint Hills prairie, Mary Smith, a 29-year-old working mother, carries a bag of groceries from her car to her house. As she walks up to the door, she sees her next-door neighbor, Dr. Tom Brown, a philosophy professor. "I'm looking forward to your class today," she calls out.

After putting the groceries away, Mary sits down at her computer and logs onto her philosophy class from New York University (in the Big Apple). She takes the daily quiz to see if she got the main points of yesterday's lecture, downloads an article in the recommended reading, and then gets into a live chat room with some of the other 1,000 students in the class and the professor teaching the course, Dr. Tom Brown, who, at this moment, is also sitting at his computer in the house next door to Mary, answering questions and posing still more.

While this illustration is fictitious today, it will soon be reality, and Mary will actually learn more by communicating with Tom via the computer than if she was sitting in his lecture class at the local university.

Whether it be continuing professional education, training for business and industry, seminars, association conferences, avocational and leisure courses, or college classes, the Internet will change the way we learn. For example:

- You will have hundreds of thousands of topics from which to choose. Want to learn about mango trees, living on Mars, brain surgery, canoeing on the Hudson River, or the presidency of James Garfield? Think of a topic — it will be offered online.
- Your teacher may be famous, but almost certainly your instructor will be the world's foremost authority in the subject. You won't settle for just any teacher.
- The number of fellow participants in your class will zoom from about 20-30 today to around 1,000 online. Even so, you'll be able to talk with the instructor more online than you can in-person today.
- You will spend about one to two hours a day learning, most of it online. Your work will demand it, but you will also enjoy personal development and fun learning online.

Photo courtesy of Revoir historical collection, Red Wing, MN

The Internet is still in an early stage of development, just like the auto at the beginning of the 20th century.

But the two biggest changes in our learning will be:

1. You and your fellow participants will form a virtual community, and you will be able to stay in touch, discuss and continue to interact with them for as long as you want.
2. How you and I learn will change dramatically. We will learn more, better, faster and more enjoyably than we do right now in the traditional classroom seminar, training or conference of today.

The Internet, while changing the way companies do business, people communicate, and consumers get entertainment, will have an even bigger impact on how we learn. It is the biggest technological invention for education in 500 years — since the invention of the printing press made printed books available to the public.

The Internet will not only change the way we learn, but it will make it better. We will be able to learn more, experience more, learn about more subjects, learn from the foremost authorities. We will also receive more personal attention, more interaction with the teacher, and get more individual feedback on how well we are doing.

Want to sit in the back of the room and daydream or write a few personal or business letters during class? Forget it. When you're online, the teacher can track the individual progress of all 1,000 students in the class.

The most important thing to understand about how the Internet will change how we learn is that this is not about children's schooling or even about college classes — this is how you and I will be learning in a few short years.

The revolution in online learning is starting and making the most advances in the area of adult learning, including continuing professional education, training for business and industry, and seminars and conferences sponsored by your national association.

But the ramifications, implications and spread of online learning will be so penetrating and irresistible that it will also change higher education, and hopefully eventually elementary schooling as well.

Let's go back to our fictitious prairie pupil, Mary Smith, because Mary is a lustful learner, not only taking a credit college course, but also involved in learning at work, and for her own personal enjoyment.

When Mary arrives at work the next day, she is pleased to learn that her employer has finally signed up everyone who works in the shop for training to improve sales and customer satisfaction. Actually, the vacuum repair shop owner has just discovered online learning himself and has gone a little overboard, registering his employees for three courses this month:

- There's an exclusive training for her employees on running a vacuum repair shop while the boss is gone, taught by a training consultant in Atlanta who has just written a book, *How to Boost Vacuum Sales and Repair While the Boss is on Vacation*. The Atlanta consultant has his own online classroom where everyone in the shop logs on for this exclusive training.
- Then there's an online seminar on customer service with 10,000 business people signed up, just $25 per person, taught by the famous author of more than 10 best-selling books on customer service, D. Vader.
- Finally, the National Vacuum Cleaner Association is having an online forum on customer service just for the vacuum cleaner sales and repair shops around the world. There will be more than 50 separate chat rooms for specific discussion topics. Mary wants to join the discussion group that is addressing the issue, "What do you say when a customer asks whether a Hoover or a Kirby is better?"

It has been a long and interesting day at the vacuum cleaner shop, but our perpetual pupil is not done learning yet. Mary has logged onto a master web site with all the online classes in the world listed there and discovered a short course on Adlai Stevenson, the Illinois politician who ran for president of the United States in 1952 and 1956. The course is sponsored by the Adlai Stevenson Historical society in Springfield, Illinois. There are 4,000 people signed up for the course, and Mary checks the participants' list — four people from Singapore, five from Seoul, and it looks like 3,000 people whose last name is Stevenson (maybe they want to know if they are related to the guy).

There are video clips, comments from some of his biographers, and an interesting anecdote from a former speech writer for Adlai Stevenson who happens to live in — Manhattan, Kansas (hey, that's interesting).

There are hundreds of thousands of people whose untapped experiences, knowledge and skills will be unleashed globally by the power of the Internet and online learning.

While these cyber anecdotes have not happened yet, enough online learning is taking place today to know that this is where it is headed. In my organization's first online course, for example, we had 300 people (10 times as many as we get at an on-site seminar). And people paid just $45 for the seminar, instead of our normal fee of $400. We made more money than ever, with fewer costs and no planes to catch.

Here's how your learning will change in the 21st century with online leaning: Geography goes from local to global. Courses and training are offered worldwide. Where you are, where the instructor is and where the course sponsor is does not matter.

Content goes from general to specific. Hundreds of thousands of topics will be offered. The global market is huge and very diverse. So instead of 500 general philosophy courses, you will be able to find "The Ethics of Theatre Productions" or "The Philosophy of Aging."

Today, a course in philosophy, customer service or computers is offered in hundreds of places. We have relatively few courses offered all over the country by hundreds of providers. When online learning hits, there will be hundreds of thousands of topics, each one offered almost continually. The result will be more choices and more options for us as learners.

Teachers aren't just knowledgeable, they are authorities. Because you will have a choice of instructors worldwide, you will tend to want online teachers who are authorities in the field, the best, most expert, in both their subject area and in presenting online.

Cost goes from high to low. The cost for all this online learning will be low, very low. Most courses will range from $25 to $99. This is because there will be so many people taking the courses.

Participation goes from around 20 to 1,000 per class. Today there's an average of 20 people in a typical continuing education class; in school and college, between 25 and 40. In an online class there will be an average of 1,000 participants.

Will This Mean Change?

Online learning will mean tremendous structural changes in our traditional educational organizations. Here are some of the changes.

Training
Training in business, which reaches only about a third of the work force, will zoom to 80 percent of the workforce. Most of it will be online training. Training experts and consultants will specialize in very specific industries and/or business processes. They will conduct their training from their homes, sometimes wearing only pajamas.

Association Conferences
The annual conference of your favorite national association will be bigger and better than ever — mainly because online participants unable to afford the travel and hotel costs will triple attendance and revenue for the conference.

Continuing Professional Education

Competition will be fierce as universities, associations, private providers and others all compete in the lucrative market of continuing professional education. There will be winners and losers — one winner to a market niche only, please. Providers will not only deliver online classes, they will also create "virtual communities" where people in the same industry or profession can chat, get news and conduct business on a daily basis at the provider's web site.

Higher Education

Colleges and universities will see dramatic restructuring. Around 50 percent of the curriculum will be online courses purchased from another college or university. That means faculty numbers will be cut in half, and most faculty will become expert in in-person teaching, leading small groups and facilitation. Worldwide authorities on faculty will teach online courses, but half of them will be located in other cities and visit the campus twice a month. With half of the curriculum delivered online, there will be need for only about half of the buildings on campus, and expensive old buildings with useless lecture halls will literally be blown up, this time by administrators.

Elementary Education

Hopefully online learning will impact elementary and secondary education for our children as well. Classrooms will be turned into carpeted discussion rooms where teachers can help children grow emotionally as well as intellectually. Online courses will free teachers to spend more time in personal, individual and small-group sessions. Fewer teachers will be needed to spend more time in personal, individual and small-group sessions. With fewer teachers, school systems will be able to afford higher salaries, better teachers and student educational attainment will go back up.

Hundreds of Thousands of Niches

The competition for teaching courses will double and triple. Each teacher and provider will choose, or try to choose, a very well-defined and targeted audience. And each online course teacher and provider will try to dominate that niche. Not just be a player, but be THE player, the ONLY source for learning for that particular group of people. There will be hundreds of thousands of topics, and hundreds of thousands of niches.

A niche might be all people interested in mango trees. A niche might be everyone interested in the life of Thomas Jefferson. A niche is not English or nursing or history. A niche is the history of France, for example. A niche might be an occupational specialty, such as home-care nurses, or secretaries to small-town doctors, or female treasurers of large corporations, and so on.

Throughout this book we use the terms "online course" and "online program." Online education will be delivered in many different formats. There will be online seminars, online training, online elementary school classes, online degree programs, online certificate programs, online conferences, and much more. To simplify, we use the generic terms online course and online program.

In their best selling book, *Positioning*, Al Ries and Jack Trout point to the three ways to become successful: be the biggest, be the best, or be there first.

Your strategy in teaching online should be to be the best online teacher for your particular niche, your topic area and your target audience. In this book we will show you how to become the best authority in your topic area.

Getting online with your particular topic first will give you a big advantage. And when you are the first and the best, then you have the best chances to be the largest online course in your topic area. This book will show you how.

Chapter 3
How Education Will Change

The driving force in society for the 21st century is the computer chip and the Internet. For the 20th century, the Industrial Age, it was the automobile and the factory that made the automobile. One hundred years ago the richest men in America were John D. Rockefeller, Andrew Carnegie and others involved in oil and steel — the stuff that made automobiles and made them go. Today the richest people in America are Bill Gates, Paul Allen and others involved in computers and the Internet.

Just like the automobile shaped society in the 20th century, the Internet will shape society in the 21st century. The automobile was not just a transportation vehicle. It created suburbs, the nuclear family, greater freedom for women, shopping malls, community colleges, consolidated school districts. And the factory that built the auto created an organizational structure based on the command and control pyramid of hierarchy. The computer chip and Internet will have a similarly dramatic and significant impact on all aspects of life in the 21st century.

We don't know yet all the ways the computer chip and Internet will influence our lives. But we do know already that the computer chip and Internet increase the need for knowledge and information. The need for current information, knowledge and knowledge skills is so great that lifelong learning will be at the center of society, including the workplace, for at least the next hundred years.

To remain competitive and profitable, every business will increasingly rely on updated knowledge and skills from its people. So we know now that lifelong learning, which has already grown tremendously in the last 25 years, will increase even more dramatically in the years ahead. Lifelong learning is the engine that runs the Information Age.

Now to understand how teaching and education will change as a result of the Internet, we go not to Bill Gates' house, not to Silicon Valley, but to Kansas, and to Frankfort, Kansas, in particular.

I have driven through Frankfort, Kansas, many times. It is about eight blocks long. There's nothing really there. There's a public school. The only store that's ever been open when we've driven through is a combination convenience store, gas station, soda grill, grocery store and youth center.

But recently my brother, who lives in Texas and frequents antique shops, found a brochure from 1909 for a department store in Frankfort, Kansas. When he gave me the brochure, I could not believe that Frankfort, Kansas, ever had a department store of this magnitude. It was called Heleker's Department Store. And it had more clothing and goods than any store that you could possibly imagine in 1900 in the town of Frankfort, Kansas, population 1,200. The store was like Nieman Marcus. There was probably not a store in Washington, D.C., or Los Angeles that had more than Heleker's in Frankfort, Kansas.

At Heleker's, they had 150 ladies' capes. They had shoes — shoes from the best line on earth. They had shoes for men, boys and youth, women, misses and children. Here's just some of the shoes they had just for infants: Baby Budd shoes; infants' silk trimmed moccasins; infants' soft solid button shoes. Now you can't buy shoes at all in Frankfort.

Soon after receiving the brochure I decided to go to Frankfort again, because I wanted to find out why there was a department store there in 1909, and what was going on in 1909 in Frankfort. So I called the library. It was closed. So I called the police station. I got an answering machine. Finally I found someone, and they told me about June, the librarian, and I called June and she invited me to the Frankfort library that afternoon.

So I came on up. The Frankfort library today is a one-room library. And I said, "I'm interested in knowing about the department store that was here in 1909." And June said, "Which one?" It turns out there were four department stores in Frankfort back then.

So I asked her what life was like in Frankfort in 1909. She said Frankfort in 1909 had six banks. It had four department stores. There were two opera houses. Frankfort had an African-American community. It had a racetrack. It had a newspaper. Not just a newspaper, but a daily newspaper. In the daily newspaper you can see the daily train schedule of the train going from Frankfort, Kansas, to New York City. The bankers were millionaires who imported marble and stained glass for their homes from Italy. It turns out there were thousands of people who came to Frankfort to do business, shop and attend cultural events.

Frankfort was a pretty special place, I thought. Well, I asked June, where was the next town that had an opera house and millionaire bankers, and she said, "Eleven miles away in Blue Rapids, Kansas."

It turns out Frankfort, Kansas, was not unique. This is how America lived. This wasn't just Frankfort. This was all of America. Because in the early 1900s, a majority of people in society farmed. We were in a rural, agrarian economy. And a large farm back then was 80 acres.

When you fly over the country, look down on the ground and you will see little squares. Those are each one square mile. It is called a section. There are 640 acres to a section. Today Kansas farms and ranches are thousands of acres. A 10,000-acre farm is not unusual.

But in the early 1900s, a farmer had 80 acres if he was lucky. And so all around Frankfort were hundreds and thousands of people who were farming, and they all came to Frankfort to buy goods, be entertained and to visit. And then something happened. They invented the automobile, and they invented gasoline. The first automobile was sold in 1896, the same year that the *Wizard of Oz* was written.

And within 10 years, Frankfort, Kansas, was in decline. The opera houses closed. Heleker's Department Store went out of business. The millionaire banker went bankrupt and went back to Scotland where he died penniless. People left town, moved to the big city, went to work in the factories.

What did Frankfort do wrong? It did nothing wrong. Instead, the automobile, gasoline, the factory and the Industrial Age changed everything about the way we live. But I don't think people woke up in 1915 and said, "My grandfather farmed. My father farmed. I think I'm going to go get a job on the factory assembly line in Kansas City or Omaha."

I don't think that's what happened. I think a more important use of gasoline-powered engines than the car was the tractor. Because the reason the largest farm was 80 acres was because that was what a horse could plow. With a tractor you could plow more, and better. You could plow 160 acres, 320 acres, 640 acres, 1,280 acres and more. And the tractor could plow deeper than a horse-drawn plow, so there was more yield per acre. Which meant there were fewer farms.

So the invention of the tractor caused people to have to move off the farm and into the cities. Today we would call it "downsizing." They had to get different jobs. And a whole way of life changed.

Think of your area of expertise, your "business" of teaching a course if you will, as an 80-acre farm. We as teachers are all running little 80-acre farms. And the tractor — in the form of the Internet — is about to change how we teach and learn.

A page from Heleker's Department Store brochure in 1907.

Beautiful

Spring and Summer

.....Suits

At $15.00 $20.00 and $25.00

You must see these suits to fully appreciate them; to catch the faultless style, the superior workmanship and fine quality of fabrics. Made of fine Panamas, in blacks, browns, blues, a complete showing of the various grays, and in mixed Novelty Cloths.

A page from Heleker's Department Store brochure in 1907.

So I tell you the story of Frankfort, Kansas, because we are all going to be impacted totally by the advent of online learning and teaching.

There will be winners and losers in teaching in the 21st century. There will be areas that grow and areas that decline.

What will grow is the number of different niches, different topic specialties, that can be taught because of the global audience made possible by the Internet. The need for in-person teachers who can facilitate a discussion, lead a group and understand people as learners will also grow.

What will decline is the number of subject-oriented teachers per subject or topic area.

Right now we have many people teaching relatively few subjects or topics. That will change. With online learning, we will see more subjects and topics taught, but each subject or topic will be taught online by only a few people.

For learners, this change will be most beneficial. In fact, the Internet will do for learning what the tractor did for food. For farmers, the invention of the tractor meant fewer and larger farms. But for consumers, for most of us, the invention of the tractor meant that food was cheaper, easier to obtain, more plentiful, and more diverse.

The Internet will make learning cheaper, easier to obtain, more plentiful and more diverse.

To be successful, you will want to find your niche in this global marketplace. You will want to move from your 80-acre farm to a much larger spread.

Chapter 4
Learning Online

Learning online is very different from attending a traditional in-person seminar. Learning online involves a totally different set of expectations, skills and behavior. And right now, in the early stages of the 21st century, online learning is still in its infancy, still imperfect, still being developed. So learning online takes a good deal of patience as well.

Currently, learning online is less expensive and less time consuming than taking a course in person. Ultimately, though, learning online will also be better than learning in person. For cognitive learning and knowledge skills, online learning will be superior to learning in person.

To teach successfully online, you will want to know as much as you can about learning online. One of the best things you can do to improve your teaching skills online is to take a course or seminar online. Here are some of the things we know now about learning online.

Traditional Lecture/Presentations

Learning online differs from traditional on-site lecture presentations. Here are some characteristics of traditional on-site lecture presentations (seminars, courses, etc.).

- It is activity based. The activity is showing up. If you show up, you have satisfied the requirements for the seminar or course (credit classes and some kinds of training are exceptions, of course).
- You don't start studying until the seminar begins. There is usually not a lot of advance work before the seminar or course starts.
- The presentation is almost totally oral. Most seminars and courses have the content presented by the teacher speaking at a certain time.
- It is held at a given time, and only at that time.

- "Discipline" is external. From the structure of the course to the time demands, they are almost always imposed from the course providers and teacher, not from the learner.
- Relative to online learning, there is less dialogue from the participants and fewer questions.
- It is a social experience. It is enjoyable. You get to meet people and discuss non-topic related items during the breaks, before and after.
- Sometimes there's food, usually coffee.
- It is a more passive experience. The instructor is very active, participants are less so.
- Quality is perceived to be the instructor's obligation. You usually evaluate the instructor or presenter. You are often not evaluated.

Characteristics of Online Learning

Here's how online learning is different.
- Content is delivered differently. It will not be given to you as a learner. In an on-site seminar or class, the teacher talks and all learners have to do is listen.
- Online, learners have to initiate learning and actively go get it. You as a learner have to figure out what you want to learn, because there is so much material. You have to read the material. You have to explore links. This takes self-direction. You also have to define your learning — what you want to learn. Others will not define it for you.
- Expect to learn via dialogue with the teacher and other participants.
- Expect to work. Learning online is work. No question about it. It is hard. It takes energy.
- Learning online is outcome and results oriented. There are "knowledge skills." There are things to know. You are here not for the process, but for the results.
- Learning online seems like it takes more time, but it actually takes less time. But you have to create the time. Be aggressive and push your schedule around, rearrange it and make the time.

You Will Feel Different

You will experience many feelings when you begin to learn online. In the beginning, those feelings won't necessarily be positive. You will feel confused, frustrated, irritated, unappreciated, lonely. You will not feel satisfied at the end of the online experience.

There are two reasons for this. First, online learning is in a primitive and early stage of development. Second, learning online has a whole different set of feelings and emotions to it than does the traditional in-person lecture/presentation. Here's what you should do.

Acknowledge the dissonance. Revel in the dissonance. Well, maybe not revel, but you can "get into" the dissonance. Recognize your feelings (to yourself, you don't have to bare your feelings to others) about learning online — it's hard, it's lonely, it takes effort, there are no smiles, there's no shopping, no dinners out on the town. Now get into it. Figure out what's going on, how you will deal with learners online when you are teaching online. Try to determine what you can best get out of an in-person traditional class or seminar. Or are you just missing the trappings of the seminar (free coffee, doughnuts if you're lucky; breaks; a chance to meet others; a chance to get out of the office).

The dissonance — the uncomfortableness, the feeling of inadequacy, of disappointment, frustration, a little depression maybe, the feeling that the teacher isn't doing it right, and that the person who set up this online course has failed miserably — that's all part of moving professionally and personally into the Information Age, into the 21st Century. You are not alone in your feelings.

Everyone feels the same way. Because we are all products of the Industrial Age, the 20th century. And now we have to learn in a totally new and different way. We don't like it. We don't know how to do it. And we can't turn back.

Techniques for Learning Online

Learning online will take some adjustments in your learning style. Following are some tips on learning online.

- Set aside a specific time during the day to participate. Learning online is asynchronous, which means you can participate anytime day or night. The "up" side of that is that you can fit your learning into your schedule. The "down" side of that is that it is easy to forget, or to try to do it while you are working. Schedule one or two hours a day to attend your online course, then do it.
- Prepare in advance. In a traditional on-site seminar, we usually don't start reading or even thinking about the subject until the seminar begins. That won't work online. With an online course, you will want to do the reading in advance. Schedule enough time before the online course to do the reading.

- It's okay if you don't know "where to go." There is no industry standard yet for an online classroom. So today there are a variety of online classrooms and formats for learning online. Until one or two online models emerge as industry standards, expect to find various formats for different online classes.
- Learn to ask questions. Online courses are actually more interactive than in-person seminars and courses. At least they can be — if you learn to ask questions. A great advantage online is your ability to ask your instructors questions and to dialogue with the other participants. This is a key learning tool. Simply being able to think out a question, phrase it and write it is a big learning accomplishment. When you are online, put aside any shyness. Don't be afraid you will look dumb (you won't). Don't be afraid you will look foolish (you won't). Ask questions. Ask lots of questions. It is one of the best learning tools ever, and online you can ask more questions than you can ever hope to in an in-person seminar.
- Dialogue with others. Communicating online can seem lonely, static and difficult. Or it can be involving, interactive, personal, even intimate. It's up to you. If you dialogue with others, create a conversation with your other participants and the instructor, you will find friends online and make your learning more personal and valuable. The key is to think of the online chat as a conversation. Don't just let someone else make a comment without responding. You would not do that in a face-to-face conversation. Instead, you would nod your head, say "yes" or "uh huh," or react with your own comment. Do the same thing online. When another person makes a comment, get in there and say "Nice comment." Or "Tell me more," or "Explain further what you mean by...."
- Test yourself. One of the wonderful new possibilities that the Internet offers your learning is tests and quizzes. You can take a quiz online. You can get the answers instantaneously without taking any of the instructor's time. The results are confidential. Take a test before the course and at the beginning of each module in the course. That will tell you how much you already know. Then after each module and at the end of the course take the quiz again to see how much you've learned. Online tests provide an objective, easily accessible, results-oriented measurement of your learning. It is the online test, not mere attendance, that will become the measurement of online learning and achievement.

Create or Respond to Modules

Your online course or seminar will likely be divided up into discrete modules. If it is not, then think of your online course in terms of modules. Each module is a separate content area. A module will be focused around a distinct concept, idea or set of knowledge skills. An online course may have from five to 10 modules. There is or could be a quiz for each module.

You can "quiz out" of those modules for which you know a lot already. This allows you to focus your attention on those modules for which you have the least knowledge. This approach speeds up your learning. It also enhances your learning because you spend your time and energy where it is needed to be spent. The quiz or test ability of the Internet allows you as a learner to find out which content areas — which modules — you have already gained sufficient knowledge about, and which content areas/modules you should study up on.

No longer do you have to "start at the beginning, go to the end" with your online learning. Now you can target your learning to those areas where you have the most interest and/or need.

Modules Lead to Other Modules

As online learning grows in availability, you will also see modules linked to other modules. Some of the other modules will be organized vertically, so that additional modules will be more "advanced," and you will see a progression in modules (for example, beginning French, intermediate French, advanced French). You will also see some horizontal module progression. For example, a person learning basic office skills will take a computer module, and then a writing or grammar module, and then a phone etiquette module, and so on. Instead of moving to "advanced" phone etiquette, the person will approach learning in a more "what's next" sequence.

Asking Questions

Learn how to ask a question online. Here are some tips:
- There are no stupid questions.
- Questions are indications you know something, not that you don't know something. Smart people ask questions. Those who know less don't ask questions.

- Use a typewriter or pen and paper to phrase your question. Give it a rough draft.
- Ask only one question at a time.
- Ask your most important question first, or the question that precedes your others. "Start at the beginning."
- Thank the person for answering your question.
- Don't be too particular to your situation. "I'm in a yellow house in a cul-de-sac, how do I..." Ask questions the teachers can answer.
- Don't be afraid to try to restate, summarize or rephrase the person's answer to confirm you understand the answer. "Let me see if I have this straight..." "So what you're saying is that..." "To put it another way..."

Talking Online

Learn to dialogue online. Talk to people in the chat room. Here are some ways to respond to others:
- Affirm. Great comment. I agree. Thanks for the new thought.
- Disagree. I see it a little differently. Isn't another way of looking at it.
- Add. Good comment. To go along with that... An additional item... To illustrate your point...
- Connect two comments from different people. Mary is saying... while Chuck is saying...
- Encourage.
- Restate. So what you're saying is...

Evaluating Your Online Learning Experience

Here are some tips on making your online learning experience a satisfactory one.
- Remember why you are taking the course online. Here are some reasons: You cannot get the subject matter locally or conveniently; you have a busy time schedule; you don't have two days to attend a seminar; the cost is less; the instructor is really good.
- Set low expectations. Online learning is in its infancy. If you are looking for the CD player in a Model-T Ford, you will be disappointed.
- Learn about online learning. See the experience both in terms of learning the content of the online seminar or course, but also in terms of learning online. Instead of trying to judge the course

overall as either good or bad, set a goal for yourself as coming out of the course saying "I learned a lot about online learning." Look for things you liked about learning online, and look for things you didn't like or you would change. This will help you in your next online learning experience.

- To learn more about online learning, teach a course yourself online. Teaching is one of the best ways to learn. And learning is one of the best ways to improve your teaching.

Summary of What You Need to Do

- Set an overall time budget. Figure out how many hours total you plan to spend on a particular online course or seminar.
- Then allocate that time budget. Figure out for each of the items below:
  1. How much time do you want to spend.
  2. What time of the day will you set aside for the particular preparation or activity regarding the online course.
- Take time to figure out your goals and objectives. Establish what you want to learn.
- Set a time to read.
- Set a time to listen to audio.
- Establish time for exploring links.
- Set a daily time for chat room dialogue.
- Be sure to allocate time to quiz or test yourself.

Learning Online is Not Right for Everyone

Learning online may not be right for everyone — right now.

In 1896 the first auto was sold. Fifty years later almost everyone traveled by car rather than horse and buggy. But it didn't happen all at once. There were auto pioneers who tolerated the flat tires, muddy roads, lack of windshields and the crank while they improved and perfected the auto. In 1896 some people decided to stick with the horse and buggy (20 years later, of course, that was not an option). Some people decided to wait to learn to drive — they would just watch for awhile and learn later. And some auto pioneers jumped right in and charged into the ditch.

Likewise with online learning, today your learners have a choice. In 20 years, online learning will constitute about 50 percent of all learning. People then will have no choice. By then online learning will seem natural. People aged 0-30 today will wonder how people learned at all before the Internet.

Here are some considerations regarding your learners options:

- If they are leaving the work force in the next five years, they don't have to learn how to learn online.
- If they are leaving the work force in the next five to 10 years, they will still have many opportunities to learn via the traditional lecture and presentation, although those options will decrease steadily.
- If they are leaving the work force in more than 10 years, they will have to know how to learn online at some time in the near future. Your learners can choose to:
  1. Wait to learn online. Learning online will improve over time. It will get better. We will figure out how it works. The technology will be perfected and standardized. Topics will proliferate. Teachers will become more experienced and expert at teaching online. Not all of your learners have to learn online right now. Some can wait.
  2. Be an online pioneer. They can jump into online learning right now. But when they do, help them not to expect someone else to have all the answers. Expect flat tires, muddy roads and no CD player, not even automatic shift. Tell them to be tough, be rugged and enjoy the ride.

If you are in the education business, as a teacher or administrator, don't try to become involved in teaching or setting up online classes without being an online learner first yourself. It won't work. As a teacher, you can't teach someone else something you haven't experienced. As an administrator, you can't develop, market or evaluate an experience you don't understand.

Chapter 5
Learning In Person

This book is about teaching online. But in order to understand the full context in which online learning will occur, it is good to know something about how people will learn in person in the 21st century.

As we have noted, about half of all learning will occur online. But that leaves the other half to be done in person. But only a small portion of in-person learning will be the traditional lecture format we have today and that characterized almost all learning in the 20th century. Traditional lecture teaching, information transfer delivered in person, will decline because it can be done more effectively online.

Most learning in person will be very different from in-person learning today. In-person learning will be focused around what the Internet cannot do. It will be oriented around the integrational aspects of learning. It will be learner-centered.

Now some learning, maybe 10-20 percent, can be done totally online. If you want to know about how to put a computer together, or maybe the history of the Civil War in the United States, you are interested in facts and data. You don't need a group discussion.

And some learning, maybe 10-20 percent, will be done entirely in person. For example, if you want to learn how to make more ethical decisions as a business manager, you don't need a lot of facts and data. Instead, you will benefit from working with a teacher and perhaps other business managers dealing with the same issue.

And there will be a large portion of learning, maybe 60-80 percent, that will best be delivered using both online learning formats combined with integrative in-person discussion learning. Using both online and in-person formats, learners will gain the cognitive knowledge and facts from teachers online, and then meet with a facilitator teacher in-person to

Projected Learning

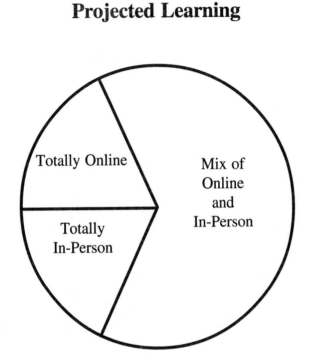

How much learning will be online during the course of the 21st century.

enhance and integrate their learning.

For example, a poetry writing class might involve an online module from a prize-winning poet, combined with an in-person class with a local poetry instructor who can review the participants' work and make more personal and individual suggestions on writing poetry.

We actually know a lot less about how people will learn in person than we do about how people will learn online. That is because online learning is almost entirely cognitive, and we have studied and practiced cognitive learning — transferring facts, information, data and knowledge — for thousands of years.

Integrative learning, the kind that will take place in person, has been practiced much less because teachers have had to spend almost all of their time on information transfer, leaving precious little time for discussions, affective learning, unlearning and other forms of integrative learning.

We can forecast that most in-person learning will take place with the participants and teacher sitting in chairs in a circle. This is the room arrangement most conducive to discussion and interaction.

And we know what we want in-person classes and meetings to accomplish. Here are some of the things that we will want in-person classes and meetings to accomplish:

- Help the participants learn how to learn.
- Encourage each learner, provide positive feedback and motivation.
- Deal with the emotions of learning.
- Help each person integrate the cognitive knowledge gained into his or her own life, the learner's own context, relevancy and meaning.
- Address the spiritual aspects of learning.
- Help learners unlearn old ideas; assist them in "grieving for their old ideas," as adult educator Jerold Apps puts it.
- Measure the integrative learning needs of the learner.
- Assess the integrative learning outcomes.
- Advise learners on their own learning directions, their best learning styles.
- Create dissonance, challenging concepts and helping to stretch individuals' minds and frames of reference.
- Help learners ask the right questions.
- Relate learning to action, assisting participants to incorporate their new-found learning into a change in behavior, either individual behavior or social change actions.
- Physically transmit a bonding between learner and other learners, or between learner and teacher, to facilitate and heighten awareness and that "teachable moment."

- Create new learning as a group that could not be accomplished individually.

I am using the term "integrative learning" to encompass all of the above. Integrative learning implies incorporating one's learning into a greater system of understanding, making sense of the knowledge, being able to master it — not simply repeat it — internalize it and use it.

The kind of teacher required for in-person learning will need to have very different skills and abilities from the kind of skills most teachers possess today. A cliche has already been created to summarize the transition: "The sage on the stage will be replaced by the guide on the side."

In-person teachers will need to know how to lead a good discussion, how to create dissonance and dialogue, how to summarize and bring things together, how to deal with the emotions of learning, how to advise learners, and most importantly, be more focused on the learners than on the subject matter. The in-person teacher will be a moderator, facilitator, advisor, counselor, broker, mentor.

The adult educator Jerry Apps has been an early pioneer in exploring this kind of learning. Here's what he says: "I emphasize an approach to teaching adults where you the teacher engage your entire personality, how you think, what you know and how you know it, and how you feel and why you feel that way. As a teacher, you ought to be prepared to help learners understand the meaning of what they are learning, help them explore and create, and help them critically analyze as well as think introspectively."

The best role model for the in-person teacher I can think of is the elementary school teacher. When my son was in grade school, each one of his teachers could sit down with his mother and myself and spend a half hour talking about my son and his learning.

There is an old saying that "Elementary school teachers love their students; high school teachers love their subject matter; and college professors love themselves." That's not nice! That's probably not fair. But it does illustrate the strengths that elementary school teachers bring to their teaching. They do not pretend to be subject experts. Instead, they are focused around helping their students to learn, and their greatest expertise is understanding the learners themselves.

You may teach a course online and not have an in-person component to the class or training. You may teach part of your course online, and then also meet with your participants in person and help facilitate their learning in person as well. Or you may market your online course to other teachers and trainers who will conduct the in-person aspect of the course or learning. All of these arrangements are possibilities. For now we will assume you are teaching a stand-alone online course or training without an in-person component to it. But it is useful to understand how in-person learning can complement and enhance the online learning.

Chapter 6
How Adults Learn

When people log on to your course for the first time, each one will come already equipped with various experiences, attitudes, perceptions and ideas. Each person will organize his or her thoughts differently, and each will be able to absorb new knowledge and ideas in his or her own way.

As we move into the era of online learning, it becomes even more important than ever to understand how we learn, so that you as a teacher can help them to learn better. As we have said before, online learning is not simply an extension of teaching the traditional lecture-oriented presentation. Online learning is not simply second best to in-person teaching. And it is not simply teaching at a distance. Online learning is an entirely different way of learning. To help your participants maximize their online learning experience, you want to know as much about how we learn as possible.

In this chapter we summarize the most important aspects of how adults learn. As an adult educator, my area of expertise and experience is primarily with adults. And adults currently constitute the largest audience and users of online learning. Not all online learning will be for adults, of course. Online learning is just as relevant and important for children, youth and students. And within a few years it will be just as prevalent in elementary and secondary schools. If your audience will be youth or children, you can adjust the following remarks to fit your audience. If your audience is young adults, many of the following characteristics of adults will be applicable in various degrees to young adults as well.

The adult's mental learning state is not a blank chalkboard on which you, the teacher, can write as you wish. Neither is the adult learner's head an empty pail for you to fill with your knowledge and ideas. The adult learner's chalkboard already has many messages on it, and his mental pail is almost full already. Your job as teacher is not to fill a tabula rasa, but to help your participants reorganize their own thoughts and skills. A prerequisite to helping adults learn is to understand how we learn.

As complex human beings, we bring to the learning situation a combined set of emotional, physical, mental and social characteristics that make each one of us unique.

Emotional Characteristics

Adults' emotional states are inextricably tied up in their ability to learn. To learn, an adult must be emotionally comfortable with the learning situation. Indeed, some educators have gone so far as to equate a good emotional state with learning. Says J. Roby Kidd in *How Adults Learn,* "Feelings are not just aids or inhibitors to learning; the goals of learning and of emotional development are parallel and sometimes identical and can probably be most conveniently stated as self-realization and self-mastery."

Throughout the ages, one's emotional state has always been manipulated to induce learning, but somehow the attempt to produce positive feelings became distorted in the mistaken belief that greater learning would occur if one produced negative feelings of pain, fear or anxiety.

The dunce cap, by way of illustration, a sign of humiliation, was not originally intended to be so. Instead, the cone-shaped headgear was believed to have magical powers, just as some contemporaries believe the similar pyramid shape has unknown powers. Putting the cap on one who had missed a question or needed help was not a punishment, but was believed to help that person learn. People in ancient cultures believed that knowledge came from heaven, and the cone shaped cap funneled knowledge into the brain. Over the years others mocked this tradition, and eventually the symbolism changed from a positive helping gesture to a sign of humiliation and ignorance.

Unfortunately vestiges of the punishment principle either consciously or unconsciously are present in even the most enlightened classes. Learning can be inhibited online in many ways. A response to a learner's comment can be condescending, corrective or dismissing, causing the learner to feel rebuked and discouraging further exploration.

In helping a person to learn, the teacher must be able to help create a positive emotional climate, and the key to that state is one's self-image.

Online, a person may have two kinds of self-image that need to be reassured. There is a person's technology self-image, as most of us do not feel technologically adequate. And there is a person's self-image as a learner.

Although most adults come to a class mentally ready to learn, at the same time they may be inhibited from learning by a less-than-self-confident learning self-image. That self-image may not be correct, may not be rational, but nevertheless exists in many if not most people. It comes from various sources.

A shy person may feel unable to participate, not wanting to disappoint the assumed expectations of others in the course. This person may "lurk" online but be reluctant to make comments. A manager who has been turned down for several promotions may feel trapped in a dead-end job and doubt the value of learning anything. A housewife who has stayed at home with children for many years may feel she is not current or informed enough to converse on an adult level again. Some who has been out of school for several decades may feel incapable of studying any more and may fear being left far behind the other students. Even educators have not taken tests in decades and may get "test anxiety" when faced with an online quiz. The causes of a less-than-positive self-image are many. They stem from natural feelings about inadequacy and growing older and some feelings that are induced artificially by society.

Physical Characteristics

Abraham Lincoln may have been able to read at night by firelight, and children may have learned in straight-backed wooden desks in drafty log cabin schools, but today's adults can detect and be influenced by the slightest changes in comfort. Adults are more attuned to comfortable surroundings, more sensitive to discomfort. This is just as true when learning online as it is for in-person classes.

All adults in your course, even the younger ones, are declining physically. Everyone is aging, even those who refuse to admit it. Our physical state affects our capacity to learn. Physique and intelligence are related because our bodies influence how and whether we can learn.

Here are some things to think about in terms of the physical aspects of learning online:

- How the light in the room falls on the computer screen, and whether there is too much or not enough light, will impact the learner's attention.
- Some computer users may not be aware of the ability to control the brightness of the screen.
- Learners online, especially those learning from their desks in their office, should close the door, notify others they are not to enter the room and reduce interruptions.

- Some people may be distracted from concentrating by their own e-mail messages that pop up and say "You have new e-mail." That message can be turned off.
- Online learners should block out a time of day for your course and be totally concentrated on learning online.
- People will learn more if they have a larger monitor. A 19-inch screen, for instance, will enhance learning over a 13-inch screen.
- Some people may want to play music while participating in an online class. Others may discover that music distracts them and reduces their ability to concentrate.
- Some learners may find they do not learn well in their offices and should unplug the computer and go home, or some other location.
- Readings viewed or downloaded from the Internet should be short and chunked.
- The more visual you can be in your presentations, the better.
- Encourage participants to have their favorite beverage handy. Even small amounts of food, like a cookie, will be helpful at certain times of the day.
- The time of day a person participates online, or studies, is critical. Every learner should determine their own peak learning times during the day, and then allocate one of them to your online class.
- Even aroma can affect learning. Some may find lighting a scented candle will enhance their experience, or putting a dab of vanilla on a nearby light bulb, or having a warm apple pie nearby, or a fire in the fireplace.

Learning online is just as much a physical experience as learning in person. Help your participants understand the impact of the physical surroundings on their online learning. They can do a lot of things to enhance their physical learning environment and improve their learning experience.

Mental Characteristics

Although adults may come to the learning situation with bodies that are not always in prime shape, the story is different for their mental attitudes. Mentally, adults are eager to learn — otherwise they would not have enrolled in your course.

Several aspects of adult learning mentality relate to your helping them to learn: a readiness to learn, problem orientation and time perspective.

A readiness to learn. Adults for the most part will come to your class ready to learn. Almost all adult learning is voluntary these days, and even societal coercion, such as peer pressure, does not seem to affect adult learners. They attend because they want to.

Part of that readiness may be a natural growth process in which "true learning" — self study, personal inquiry, or self-directed learning — is more welcome after one's formal schooling or education ends. Even the 16th century master of self-study, Montaigne, wrote about his education, "At 13, I had completed my course, and in truth, without any benefit that I can now take into account."

Whether their experiences in school were beneficial or not so positive, adults want to view their adult learning experiences as separate from more formal schooling and will approach them differently. This may be because adults are not only ready to learn but need to learn.

Problem orientation. Education for children is often subject-centered, concentrating on various disciplines like philosophy and science, and the abstract as well as the practical. Adult learning, on the other hand, is more problem-centered. Adults want to learn to solve or address a particular problem and are more satisfied with their learning if it applies to their everyday experiences, is practical or is current.

Adults are oriented toward problem-solving because they are faced with certain developmental tasks stemming from the roles they assume, or want to assume, in their families, work and society. These tasks and roles demand a good deal of adjustment, accomplishment and learning. Although society pushes few adults into the classroom, it certainly creates enough needs and wants to encourage adults to perform their best in various roles and life stages.

Time perspective. Another and related impetus for problem-orientation in adult learning is that an adult's time perspective is different from that of children. As a child, time, both past and future, is a vast quantity. A year ago is a long time. And the future is endless. Increasingly, as one becomes older, time becomes less expendable and more limited. The future is not so endless after all, and the past blurs a little so that 10 years wasn't all that long ago. As time becomes more limited, it becomes more important. In the learning situation, adults prefer what can be learned today or in the near future to what can be learned over a longer period of time. The adults' interest in solving problems within their older time perspective makes adults more concerned with specific, narrow topics of relevance than broad, generalized or abstract subjects.

A readiness to learn, problem orientation and specific time perspective contribute to an internal motivation to learn.

The time and problem orientations do not imply that everything adults want to learn is so immediate as fixing the plumbing. Many different kinds of issues, thoughts and ideas may constitute a timely problem. For one person, finding out whether beauty lies in a museum painting or in a mountain-top view may constitute a legitimate learning problem. For another person determining how the ancient philosophers combined work with study may be an equally immediate problem.

Social Characteristics

The most important social characteristic of the adult learner is an abundance and variety of experiences. This aspect alone makes teaching adults different from teaching children.

Your participants will be coming from different backgrounds, occupations or occupational specialities, types of upbringing, ethnic heritages, and income levels. Each one will have a different mix of experiences and previously formed perceptions when entering your online course. Some of these perceptions are about school, group interactions, and the subject.

School. Even if you are not working in a school-like atmosphere, structured learning situations are inevitably associated with previous schooling. For many people their formal schooling was less than successful. Many adults received low grades in school and have some stigma attached to that period of time. Others may have outwardly done well in school, but inwardly felt the experience was boring or a waste of time. Generally speaking, it is best to reduce the number of associations with formal schooling in your references, style and approach to the subject. When teaching those with unfavorable school experiences, it is wise not to repeat those mannerisms and actions that may remind your participants of their past situations. The imprint of our schooling is still on all of us, and if those memories are not good, it is best not to revive them.

Group interactions. Your online class is a group experience. And it is just one kind of group in which adults participate. Some will come with positive expectations about interacting in a group; some will not. Some will come wanting to be leaders in the group; others will have already decided before your online course starts to be passive or take a minimal role in group participation. Some will see the group as an opportunity to display talent and knowledge while others will see it as a possible threat to exposing their lack of talent and knowledge.

The subject. Every adult coming to your online course will have some perception about the subject to be discussed. Some will have a degree of proficiency in the topic; others will have been acquainted more superficially. Some will have had a negative encounter with the topic, or gained some misinformation. Others will have thought about it without personal experience, and come with curiosity and some ideas not based on reality but on what others have said or done.

Social psychologist Gardner Murphy says that adults, contrary to common assumption, are not able to detach themselves emotionally from the subject at hand. "The adult has not fewer but more emotional associations with factual material than do children, although we usually assume that he has less," he says.

Working with your participants' experiences is perhaps your most rewarding challenge. This is particularly true online, as you have the ability to tap into all your participants' thoughts online.

These varied and copious experiences need to be handled on two levels. First, you as a teacher need to deal with the backgrounds your participants bring to your online course. If someone has some misinformation about the subject, you will need to clarify and help that person "unlearn." If some of your participants automatically shy away from making comments online, you may want to try to draw them out or structure safe and comfortable exercises to help them interact as much as possible.

On another level, you have an abundant resource at hand in the past experiences of class members. Each has some event, skill, idea or knowledge worth sharing with the rest of the group. As Sharon Merriam and Rosemary Caferella note, "Life experience functions in several ways... Adults call upon their past experiences in the formulation of learning activities, as well as serving as one another's resources in a learning event." Online, you can tap into your participants' experiences and ideas in an exponentially greater fashion than you can ever do in an in-person class.

You can establish subgroups of participants by particular interest area or experience. You can have each person post comments, remarks and writings. You can call upon participants in different locations or with different perspectives for input. You can ask participants to respond to others' questions and help them teach each other.

Tap into the variety in backgrounds to illustrate your points. Encourage discussion. Stimulate peer teaching. And gain new knowledge yourself. It is this wealth of experience, ideas and knowledge in your participants that makes teaching adults so exciting and rewarding. Drawing on your participants' experiences can make the online class an exciting and new experience every time you teach; to ignore the past experiences of your learners is to miss out on something valuable and special.

Motivation

The total of one's mental, emotional, physical and social states determines a person's motivation to learn. Much attention throughout history has been paid to how to motivate people. Generals have tried to motivate troops, supervisors have tried to motivate workers, salespeople have tried to motivate themselves, staffs have tried to motivate boards of directors, and boards of directors have tried to motivate staffs.

The quest for motivation has led to much thought on the subject as well. Those writing about the power of positive thinking can stay on the best seller list for weeks or even years, and those speaking about it can fill halls with rallies on motivation.

Most authorities on adult learning advocate encouraging self-directed learning. For example, author Laurent Daloz says, "We teachers sometimes speak of pushing our students to higher stages of development. We want the best for them after all, and need to know that we have made a difference in their lives, an important difference. To push a person to change is about as effective in the long run as trying to push a chain uphill. People develop best under their own power."

As a teacher, you will doubtless be confronted by people with a range of motivations, from those so highly motivated you will be reluctant to give them your e-mail address or home phone number, to those who will seem inert and lifeless and unreceptive to anything you say or any way you say it.

In online learning, self motivation is even more essential than in-person learning. The requirement for self motivation and self discipline is built into online learning and the whole fabric of life in the 21st century. Ultimately, it is the individual's responsibility to learn. You can and should help the person's attempts to learn. You also have the power to hinder a person's ability to learn. By failing to recognize limits, by ignoring or even constructing barriers, by not understanding how a person learns, you can be a negative influence on someone's learning. By facilitating learning and helping your participants, you can be a positive influence.

Part II.
Planning Your
Online Course

Chapter 7
The Economics
of Online Courses

Your online course is not just an educational experience, it is also an economic activity. For the past hundred years, educational activities took place within the paradigms and parameters of the Industrial Age. Those economic paradigms and parameters are changing as we move further into the Information Age. So it will be increasingly difficult to make your online course be successful using the assumptions and rules of the last century. Increasingly, you will need to position your online course using the rules of the Information Age. Here are some of the economic principles of the Information Age.

The Shift from Products to Markets

In The *One to One Future,* the best marketing book of the last decade, business authors Don Peppers and Martha Rogers urge us to "manage your customers, not just your products."

"In the traditional marketing organization, products are managed, and customers are simply counted at the cash register."

They recommend we stop managing products — courses, seminars and other educational programs. Instead Peppers and Rogers suggest we manage customers — participants, learners and students. Here's why.

In the old world of the 20th century, we had a product orientation. We start with a course and then we offer this course to people. The problem with this scheme is that the real force here is people, our markets, our target audiences.

With a product orientation, we are unable to foresee, plan and adjust our programs to the changing interests and demands of our learners. We will only know it when enrollments decline. And then we won't know why.

In today's world, we have a people orientation. We start with our markets, our target audiences. Then we build courses around each different market segment. In this way, we become responsive to our learners, to people instead of programs. We are then better able to do research, listen to our customers, understand their needs and adjust our offerings accordingly. We are also able to go after new audiences and look for new opportunities.

Segment Your Audience

"We serve everyone" is no longer a successful way to look at your potential audience. When someone asks you who would be interested in your course and you answer, "Anyone," that is a risky proposition.

It assumes there is one audience, one general public. But audiences are being defined in more specific terms, more distinct from each other, more defined by demographic characteristics than ever before. So there is not one audience, there are many.

There are no longer "nurses." There are now rural school nurses, emergency room nurses, large hospital nurses, small hospital nurses. Every audience is being divided up into ever-smaller segments.

In order to offer your online course successfully, you will want to define your audience by segment. That means using some kinds of demographics to define the people who will be most interested in your online course.

Here are some of the most commonly used demographic variables used to define target audiences today: geography, age, occupation, education level, job title, size of company, sex.

Look at the demographic characteristics of the people presently enrolled in your courses, who are your current customers, or are members of your organization already. These are most likely the characteristics of your potential participants in your next online course.

Look at several different market segments in choosing what audiences you want to target.

Traditional Boundaries are Disappearing

The traditional boundaries between organizations and businesses are disappearing. The Internet has destroyed these boundaries.

Geography is no longer a boundary. It used to be that your organization, your business, was defined by your city, your county, your state, your region or your country. You may still define it by geographic boundaries. But others on the Internet do not recognize geographic boundaries. They will serve anyone, anywhere. Geography will no longer protect your course from the competition.

Time and place are no longer boundaries. Along with geography, time and place used to be boundaries. We would offer something that is convenient to our customers. We were closer to our customers. We were more available. Today, with the Internet being open 24 hours a day, 365 days a year, anyone on the Internet can be accessible to anyone much more easily than a physical location can be convenient. Time and place are no longer advantages to you.

Affiliation is no longer a boundary. It used to be if you were a doctor, you were a member of the association of doctors. If you were a Methodist, you went to the Methodist Church. No longer. People feel less bound by tradition to belong, patronize or be loyal to organizations and businesses that have traditionally served them. If they can be served better by some other organization or business, they will shift their loyalty and participation to the other entity serving their current needs. Just because you are involved in serving a particular audience, that does not mean they have to or will necessarily come to you for their online learning. You will need to establish your credibility and service to them all over again.

Education Has to be Financially Self-Sufficient

More and more, educational activities such as your online course have to be financially self-sufficient or even make money. Even though you may just be the teacher and not be concerned with the finances of the organization sponsoring your online course, you will want to understand the economics of courses in the Information Age.

Fewer and fewer educational activities can be subsidized or funded. More and more educational activities have to generate sufficient income through registration fees and other means in order to sustain them financially. Here are the financial components of an educational activity:

- **Income.** This is usually from registration fees, although it could be funded, donations or other sources of income.
- **Promotion.** This is a cost. Many educational activities require some kind of marketing or promotion to generate participation and enrollments.
- **Production.** These costs include handouts, materials, and most of all, your fee as a teacher.
- **Administrative.** If your course is sponsored by an organization, there will be additional costs to pay for administrative staff and overhead and to support the sponsoring organization.
- **Net profit.** Some courses may need to generate a net profit for the sponsoring organization.

Promotion is Increasing, Other Costs Declining

In the last century, promotion costs were low, production costs were high, administrative costs were high, and net profits were low for most educational activities. That formula has to change for educational activities to exist successfully in the 21st century. Here's how that will change:

- Promotion costs go up. Marketing and promotion costs will continue to grow as a percentage of income. There is simply too much supply, and too many choices for people in their buying. To capture your market, more promotion will be necessary.
- Net profits go up. In order to remain competitive and have the funds for future success, organizations, companies and even individuals have to have higher profits. Educational activities are receiving less outside funding. Outside funding will continue to decline. So educational activities, including your online course, will need to make money at some point.
- Administrative costs go down. In order for promotion and net profits to go up, something has to go down. Administrative costs need to go down.
- Production costs go down. As a percentage of income, production costs have to go down. This impacts you because your pay as a teacher is part of production costs. Your pay does not have to go down as a dollar figure, only as a percentage. That is one reason why we advocate online course enrollments with large numbers, so that more income can be generated and you as a teacher can still receive adequate or good payment for your services.

New World

Instead of using the boundaries of geography, time, and affiliation, organizations must now position themselves to take advantage of a global niche.

These relative movements in promotion, production, administration and net profit are valid for most all information service industries, not just educational activities. They are simply the requirements for economic success in the coming century.

Now let's relate these new economic rules to your online course. Many current online courses are operated on the principles of the last century. They have high production, low promotion and low net profit margins.

A typical online course might have 20 students and charge $500 or so per course. The high price holds down enrollments and income. There are high production costs, and therefore little left over for net profit.

Price pressure is already driving down online course fees. As more people and organizations offer more online courses, the price of an online course will continue to fall.

To gain an advantage, courses will need to have more promotion and marketing. That will be justified if enrollments go up. With larger enrollments, there can be a bigger income for the online course even with lower prices. The new economic environment will call for lower prices and larger numbers of participants. By being able to teach 100 or more participants online, you will be able to make your online course successful financially.

Chapter 8
What an Online Classroom Looks Like

With the area of online programming still very new, some things have not been decided yet. One of those undecided things is what an online classroom looks like.

In the next few years various models of online classrooms will be developed, and eventually some models will gain greater acceptance and usage than others.

Currently, most online classrooms are textual in nature, with words and buttons to get from one area to another. Few are very visual in nature. That will probably change, as more online classrooms become more visual and graphical.

The technology of online classrooms have three stages of development: written and graphic; audio, and video.

Written and Graphic Technology

Written and graphic technology is available and in use. It is also almost always technically available to anyone who can access the Internet, so your target audience and participants should be easily able to use written and graphic technology without any extra hardware or software.

Written and graphic technology may also be the most important technology from the point of view of how the Internet will change learning. Most of the changes in how we learn may very well come from the innovations and opportunities available over the Internet in written and graphic capabilities.

Here is a list of most of the written and graphic capabilities for online learning:

1. Text, lecture notes, instructional presentation. The presenter or instructor can upload her or his lecture notes, text or instructional presentation and make it available to all participants at any time they want to access it.

One advantage from a marketing point of view is that the participant does not need to take notes but can download and print any of the presenter's information. Another key marketing point in promotion is that the participant can view, or review, the material anytime she or he wants and at the pace, intensity and time commitment that the learner wants.

2. Readings. Related text and lecture notes, readings, references, articles and other information for which distribution permission has been granted can be uploaded and made available to participants.

An advantage of this feature from a marketing point of view is the significant reduction in the cost of producing the program. Much more information can be made available to participants on your web site than can be mailed or sent. And it costs your organization nothing in reproducing and mailing costs to upload the readings, so your costs are cut. Maybe more importantly, costly staff time spent mailing readings and information is reduced or eliminated.

3. Links to other web sites. Providing links to other web sites and information is a delightful plus in online learning. The links can be in a reference section, but they can also be integrated into the class material and even online discussions or chats.

For example, many college credit courses establish a relationship with an online library so students in the course can have access to a wealth of other reading materials.

Another illustration is that the instructor or participants can reference a technique, drawing, quote or explanation on another web site and invite the rest of the participants to click on the address to see the reference immediately.

For marketing purposes, we have not begun to explore fully the variety and depth of uses that links to other web sites can provide. For example, the participants' list could contain links to the participants' individual home pages with information about each participant, his or her interests, history, and so on that will be a valuable networking and peer learning tool. Such links will give each participant far more information about the other participants than is currently available during in-person introductions.

4. E-mail. E-mail capabilities give the instructor and individual participants the opportunity to communicate directly, personally and confidentially. This one-to-one communication allows participants to ask questions and may lessen the reticence of some participants to venture forward with so-called "stupid" questions, thus encouraging more people to ask more questions. This capability actually expands a presenter's physical ability to respond to questions — that is, the instructor can actually answer more questions using e-mail than the instructor could in-person. Internet guru Leonard Charnoff estimates an instructor can answer 200 questions a day, with each answer individually written and tailored. Since experience suggests that learners ask the same questions over and over again, instructors could write a prepared response to the most commonly asked questions, giving the instructor the ability to answer even more questions individually.

While much question and answer discussion is more beneficial in a group online setting, nevertheless e-mail also gives the instructor the opportunity to deal with sensitive, remedial or individual learning styles when an individual response is desired.

5. Asynchronous chat rooms. One of the truly remarkable and breakthrough technologies provided by the Internet is the opportunity to have an asynchronous group discussion using what is called a "chat room" or "discussion forum."

The technology allows any participant and the instructors to submit written comments, questions and responses to the discussion forum, where everyone can read the comments.

"Asynchronous" means that the comments submitted do not have be done at a given time, and that people can read them no matter what time of day they log into the discussion.

From the marketing perspective, the asynchronous nature of the discussion opens up global opportunities for participation and increased registrations, income and profits.

Because people can and do participate at any time of the day (a day meaning a 24-hour period, not daylight or work day), people from all over the world can participate in your online program. This opens up enormous marketing potential. A second tremendous marketing opportunity is that even participants in the same time zone do not have to participate at the same time, thus an individual can participate in your online program anytime during the day or night she or he wants or has available.

Another opportunity from a marketing point of view is that individuals can review what was said the prior day, previous week or even past month as chat room dialogue can be archived and saved. This gives participants an opportunity to catch up on what they missed, and an opportunity to gain a written transcript of the conversation for future review and learning.

There are more marketing advantages of the asynchronous chat room, and undoubtedly additional ones will be discovered. The asynchronous discussion forum is a distinctive, unique feature of online learning that gives online programming a significant marketing edge.

6. Live chat rooms. Live chat rooms allow a given number of people to engage in a written group discussion live. The actual number of people allowed varies according to the software program used.

This has the advantage of more immediacy, less waiting time, more spontaneity in dialogue. It is more difficult for people in various time zones to participate, and for the most part participants have to be committed to a specific time of day for the discussion. To have a live chat room, the sponsoring organization needs to have IRC program established, a software program called "Internet Relay Chat," or some equivalent. Participants also have to have some kind of software added to their computer's capability, usually downloaded off the Internet, as well.

7. Threaded bulletin boards. Another software used extensively on web sites is the threaded bulletin board. This is a versatile software tool that can be used for messages, reports and other postings of information.

8. Quizzes, tests and exams. Another defining and unique advantage of online programming is that participants can take quizzes, tests and exams. This technology can be used in several ways.

A) Learners can test themselves without other participants knowing their scores or even the instructor knowing the person's score. This capability enhances self directed learning and measuring learning without imposing any feelings of inadequacy on the part of the learner.

Thus, a daily quiz could be created by the instructor and participants could test their progress daily. Or potential participants in your online program could test themselves in advance of the program to see if the program material is too advanced, too elementary, or just right for them.

B) Instructors can gain access to a participant's test scores. If the test is set up so that the instructor can have access to the participant's test scores, then the instructor can aid the participant in his or her progress in the program. This would allow the instructor to provide specific recommendations for each learner.

C) Surveys can be conducted. Surveys can be taken on a daily basis and that information can aid in the instruction of online programs. Opinions, behavior and other things can be surveyed and the results tallied and posted almost immediately, so that all participants can see the results.

While the opportunity of testing may vary according to the type of online program you are offering, there are many positive marketing advantages to having these capabilities in an online program.

Audio Online Technology

The technology for written information transfer and chat room discussion is currently available and very exciting, allowing for interaction, information delivery and discussion. Adding to the capabilities of the Internet is audio.

Audio is delivered in two ways:

1. Recorded tapes that can be downloaded to your computer and then played whenever you want.
2. Live, real-time audio like radio.

The recorded audio, like tapes and cassettes, can be stored on your web site. You can have as many as you want. A person downloads a particular tape and then listens. The main consideration at this time with audio tapes is whether or not the majority of your participants will have sound cards and the technical capability to download the tapes. If they do, audio tapes are a great resource. The most obvious use of tapes would be for the teacher to tape her or his presentations so that participants can listen to the lectures. Another possibility is for the instructor to interview or have a discussion with another resource person and to tape the conversation. As people learn in different ways, having the audio capability will be an enhancement to the learning process.

Live, real-time audio involves a more complex and costly kind of technology. It will be useful for cybercasting conferences and other live events where the "here and now" is more important than a class lecture. At some point it will be possible for instructors to broadcast their lectures over the Internet in real time and tape them for future replay by participants who were not able to hear the original delivery.

Whether taped or live, audio provides another enhancement to the learning power of the Internet. At the time of this writing, audio was becoming widely available and widely used. The technology for the user involves getting or purchasing audio software, such as Real Audio.

Video

Coming at some point in time will be video. There are video programs on the Internet at the time of this writing, but the quality is much lower than most learners would expect in a course situation. But video is not necessary for online learning to happen. The written, chat room and audio capabilities currently available are more than enough technology to deliver a successful class or seminar over the Internet. Do not wait for video to conduct your online course.

The video capability involves a "larger tube" in technical capacity for the Internet and thus will take some time before the engineers of the Internet can build that larger tube to carry video.

Video will allow you to see the instructor. Eventually it will allow the instructor to see you as well. This will have some positive benefits in group discussion and interaction.

But in our television-oriented culture, the benefits of video to learning over the Internet may be overrated. Much learning can already take place with written, discussion forum and audio technology.

Online course delivery is not dependent on video for success. You should not wait for video to begin your online course delivery. The video technology for the Internet will be developed by the for-profit sector sooner or later. When video does come to the Internet, it will be an enhancement, not a replacement, to what you have already built.

The LERN Model for an Online Classroom

My organization, the Learning Resources Network (LERN), has developed an online classroom, which for our purposes here can serve as an illustration of what an online classroom looks like. It has been successfully used by our association.

If you want to see it on the Internet, go to *www.lern.org* and check out the "Education Center" from our home page.

At the time of the online event, participants go to the Education Center on our web site and then go to the LERN Online Classroom, where they enter the password given to them at the time of registration. When they enter the LERN online classroom they find:

- <u>Welcome</u> — where the online course agenda is posted, along with instructions on how to participate.
- <u>Presentation Hall</u> — an asynchronous chat room or discussion forum where the presenters provide information and answer questions

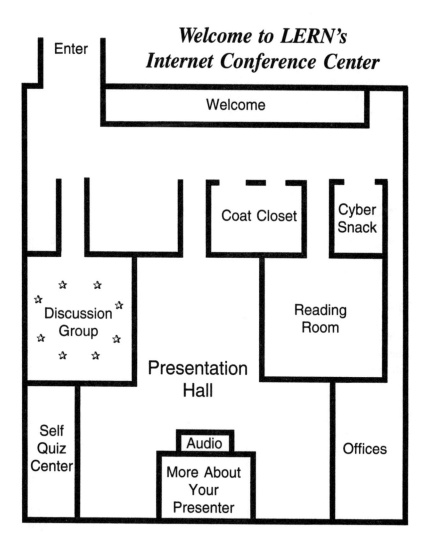

This is one model for what an online classroom looks like. It was designed by LERN and is used for our online seminars and courses.

several times during the day. Participants also make comments here directed toward the presenters.

- Discussion Group — an asynchronous chat room or discussion forum where participants discuss whatever they want and answer questions posed by the presenters.
- Audio — participants can download audio cassettes of talks or lectures by the presenters.
- Reading Room — participants can download readings or other material posted there by the presenters.
- Quiz Center — participants can take self quizzes to see how well they are progressing.
- Live Chat Room — at certain times a live chat room will be available with the presenters.
- Coat Closet — a listing of all the participants so people can see who else is attending the event.
- Cybersnack — a cartoon, updated during the week, for a little break.

Technical Aspects of Teaching Online

Here we have provided a non-technical overview of what constitutes an online classroom. Throughout this book, technical questions will come to your mind about how to accomplish a given task or activity on the Internet.

This book is non-technical in nature. It is non-technical primarily because teaching online involves more educational skills than technical skills. It is also non-technical for two other reasons:

- The pedagogical (teaching) and andragogical (learning) changes in online learning are so profound that focusing this book on the educational aspects of teaching online is really more important than the technical aspects of teaching online.
- Technical changes quickly. Every year, every month, every week, it seems the technology of the Internet changes. Anything we could say about technology would be valid for only a few months after the book was published.

Some of you may want to learn the technical aspects of Internet software, programming and running a web site. But you do not have to know much of anything about technology in order to teach online. In fact, if you try to keep abreast of the technology changes related to the Internet you might not have any time left over to stay current in your field of interest.

So I would recommend the majority of you utilize the knowledge and resources of a webmaster, web developer, or computer expert. Let them do the technology; you stick with the teaching. Technical expertise does not necessarily have to be expensive. You can contract out with a college student who will work with you part time. Even many high school students have a high degree of technical expertise on the Internet. You can work with an institution or organization that has those capabilities in-house already. Or you can barter with a person or organization and trade your skills for those of the technology person. You can always purchase technical expertise from the myriad companies that offer their services in this area.

Online Classroom Vendors

There are a number of companies which provide online classroom software for teachers and organizations conducting online courses. At the time of this writing, the Learning Resources Network (LERN) recommends the following:

- Education To Go, Temecula, CA
  Contact Jules Ruggles at jruggles@educationtogo.com, 909-698-2264, www.educationtogo.com.
- eCollege, Denver, CO
  Contact the sales office at info@ecollege.com, 303-873-7400, www.ecollege.com.
- University Online Publishing, McLean, VA
  Contact the sales office at info@uol.com, 703-893-7800, www.uol.com.
- AppsToGo, Minneapolis, MN
  Contact Cem Erdem at info@appstogo.com , 612-914-6697, http://appstogo.com.

Chapter 9
Planning Your Online Course

In the new environment of the Information Age and the 21st century in which you will be teaching, you will also want to be a marketer of your course. In the old world, you just taught. You didn't worry about getting people to come to your class. Somebody else worried about that. But the marketing of your online course in the new environment is critical. If you do not position your online course properly in the very competitive environment out there, you will not have a long term online success.

There are two absolutely critical aspects of a successful online course that you as teacher have to get right. One is the topic or subject area you will teach. The other critical aspect you have to get right is the target audience.

Choose Your Audience

In planning a successful online course, the beginning and the end — the alpha and the omega — of success will be the list of names of people you want to attend your program.

The list is everything. Show me the names!

Do not expect to be able to post your course with search engines and have people show up. Do not pretend that your course is for everyone. Do not even think that lots of administrators will be begging you to teach for them. And do not think, pretend or expect someone else to do the marketing of your online course for you.

In the new environment, marketing comes first. Teaching comes second. If you have the market, you can deliver the program. If you don't have the market, you don't have anything.

For most all online courses, advertising is out of the question. And publicity is hard to get. That leaves the best, most cost efficient and most effective way of promoting your course — direct marketing. Direct marketing involves getting a list of potential participants in your course and then marketing specifically to that list.

So the objective is to define your target audience so clearly and specifically that you can produce the list of names of people in your target audience.

You identify the interest or need that everyone in the list shares. And the interest or need matches your teaching expertise.

Long-term strategy is even more important than short-term success in online course success, because online programming is here to stay. If you can capture the market, you can keep the market. So long term, begin thinking of your audience less in geographic terms and more in terms of interest and need. Think globally.

So if you are a hospital consultant in Maryland, think less of your audience as the hospitals in Maryland, and more in terms of the hospitals in North America. Then think about every hospital in the world. Then think of every hospital in the world with a specific interest or need that matches your expertise. There's your list.

Here are some ballpark numbers. Your universe — your total potential audience — should be at least 1,000 people, and top out at around 10,000 people. If you have more than 10,000 people, you likely have more than one target audience. Now these are not just people in the world, these are names you can acquire. It is like the tree that falls in the forest and you don't hear it. If you can't get the names, they really don't exist.

The place to start in defining your online audience is with your current participants, students, members or customers. For some situations, your customers may be institutions or organizations. This is your core. Build on it. Go after people who look just like your current audience.

You already have a core group of supporters. They already have a positive image of you. You already deliver something of great value to them. This is where to start. This is the foundation upon which you build.

Do not think of going after a totally new audience. Do not think about renting e-mail lists. Do not think about chasing untested and untried lists of names. Develop something very successful for your existing audience. In particular, develop something very successful for your existing audience on the broadest geographical scale possible. Then acquire names of people with the same demographic characteristics as your core present participants.

If you do not choose your target audience, you will not capture your target audience. If you do not capture your target audience, you will lose out to someone else who has more clearly defined her or his audience, and then delivered the kind of online courses that audience wants. As soon as you capture your audience, you can keep your audience. It will be very hard for someone else to take it away from you. So choose your target audience wisely.

Choose the Course Topic

Here are the best measures of success for a topic for an online course:
- Narrow and specific in scope
- Not offered by the competition
- Not offered on-site or in-person
- Compelling, high interest
- Difficult or costly to hear the instructor/s in person

Narrow and Specific in Scope

Whatever you offer online should be an offering that you want to be known for, that strengthens your professional image, and that will assist you in dominating your knowledge niche.

So the subject areas you want to focus on are those in which you excel, your main bread-and-butter subject areas with your target audience.

Within the subject areas that match your expertise, narrow the subject area down to a topic that is very narrow and specific in scope. What is "very narrow and specific in scope" will vary according to your target audience. If you are an historian in Australia and teaching a history course to North Americans, the "History of Australia" would be a topic narrow and specific in scope. If you are teaching a history course for Australians, however, the "History of Australia" would NOT be narrow and specific in scope. The "History of Melbourne" might qualify.

Not Offered by the Competition

Welcome to the new world of teaching. It is a world in which you as a teacher have competition. In fact, you have nothing but competition. Everyone out there is an expert. Everyone is a professor. Everyone thinks he knows more about your subject area than you do. It is likely that long term there will be only one to three online courses surviving per topic or subject area. The teacher with the most participants will lower the course price to get even more participants, and that teacher will capture the market. So you will need to deal with other online courses and teachers as competition.

You can offer the same courses and programs as is offered by the competition, but it will have a far lesser chance of success than if you offer programs not offered by the competition.

When we talk about "same program" we do not mean the same broad subject area. If your competition offers an online program on computers, that doesn't mean you should avoid offering a computer course online. It does mean you should find a different angle, perspective, sub-specialty or some other distinction that will make your online program different.

Not Offered In-Person or On-Site

One way to enhance your success is to offer topics that your audience cannot get from in-person or on-site seminars or courses. You can have a successful online program competing with an in-person program, but steering clear from in-person program topics will just give you another edge and another opportunity for greater success.

Twenty years from now, all types of subjects and topics will be offered online. But right now, there is a very definite rationale in not competing against a program that is offered in-person or on-site, even or especially if it is offered by your own organization.

The reason is simply that online programs are new and different and our audiences are not used to them. So familiarity and inertia will dictate that many people will opt for the program in person or on-site.

But if the only way I can get this program is online, then more people will risk the unfamiliarity of online learning because they want so much to learn what you have to offer.

Compelling and High Interest

You can succeed with a program title that is not necessarily compelling or showing high interest with your target audience. But having a compelling and high interest topic will, once again, enhance your chances for success online.

So if there is a "hot" topic with your audience, a current topic area that has just arrived or a big problem or concern with your audience, find your online program topic there.

Difficult to Hear the Presenter/Instructor In Person

Another way to position your online program for greater success is to promote it to people who cannot hear you in person. And a big bonus to increase online course success is to line up one or more co-presenters or co-instructors not available to your audience for in-person or on-site programs.

The person or persons may not be available for on-site or in-person programs because 1) The travel distance is too great; 2) The person has a busy schedule; or 3) Your audience could not afford what you would have to charge for this person.

For whatever reason, if you can line up an otherwise unavailable presenter or instructor, even for a day, to teach or present online, you will enhance your online program's chances of success.

Not every successful topic has to meet all of the above criteria. Each of the above will give you an additional edge, pull in a few more people, and make it all that much easier for you to score a success with your online programming.

The more advantages your online program has, the more reasons you can give your audience to take your online program, the better your chances of success.

Choosing Your Expertise

At the same time as you are choosing the title, topic or subject area of your online course, you are choosing your area of expertise. Now you may think you already have an area of expertise, you don't need to choose it again.

But in the new world of learning, you will indeed need to choose your area of expertise all over again. Here's why. In the old world of the Industrial Age, which is in decline and will continue to fade, geography was a main determinant of boundaries. That is, you could be the best darn customer service expert in the tri-county area, and that was fine. That nasty big time customer service author on the coast was so far away he didn't care about invading your tri-county area. But that's all changed. Today that big time customer service expert can reach your clientele in your tri-county area online.

You no longer have geography as an advantage, or as a defense. To be successful teaching online, you will want to choose an area of expertise in which you can become the foremost authority — even better than that rich author on the coast.

So you will want to become an authority. You should be the best, the foremost authority, the top gun, the best expert, the guru — in whatever you are teaching.

There is no room for the average teacher, the good teacher, the nice guy presenter, the best available presenter in the tri-county area. There is only room for authorities, for the best instructors in the world. Because if you don't have the authority, then someone else does, and then they own your niche. Because why would someone want to take a course from anyone other than the best authority in the world? They don't, they won't.

Some Illustrations

- If Alan Dershowitz, the famous lawyer from Harvard, is hired by an organization to teach his specialty of law, that organization will own its niche. There will be few, if any, attorneys who will want to take the same course from the law professor at Singapore State, as nice as that person is, as great a teacher as that person is. If Alan Dershowitz is a lousy teacher, of course, he loses. But if he is the best, everyone else loses. UNLESS the law professor at Singapore State is an expert in something else — like why Alan Dershowitz is wrong — or has a subspecialty in law — the law of engineering in the state of Wyoming — that Alan Dershowitz doesn't. Then the law professor from Singapore State isn't competing with Alan Dershowitz. She is the world's best expert in another topic, appealing to another niche.
- If you are taking a course on the presidency of Grover Cleveland, you want the best biographer and historian of President Cleveland as your teacher.
- If you are interested in learning about mango trees, you want the foremost authority on mango trees to teach it.

Up until now, instructors could compete offering the same course because of geography (a teacher could not be in New York and Los Angeles at the same time); and because of time (an instructor can teach only so many classes on Tuesday morning). Now those boundaries are gone. The world will need only one good course per topic, because anyone in the world can take the course. And because it is offered on demand, up to 24 hours a day, 7 days a week, so anyone can take it any time.

So you will need to be the foremost authority on whatever topic or subject you teach online. Now I will show you how to become the foremost authority in the world.

How to Become the Foremost Authority

In the next few pages, I will show you how to become the world's foremost authority.

While I'm at it, I can also show you how to become the richest person in town. Having lived in Kansas for more than 20 years, I spent a lot of time driving through the beautiful Flint Hills of Kansas, with wide open places, few people and very small towns. It was then it occurred to me how to become the richest person in town. You move to a town which is small enough, and poor enough, that you become the richest person in town. To become the world's foremost authority, you follow the same guidelines.

Here's another illustration. My wife grew up in a town of just 400 people. When she was a little girl, she thought her father was famous. And she had proof — everyone in town knew him.

You can turn yourself into the foremost authority in the world. Here's how. Choose a topic area narrow and specific enough that you are the foremost authority in the world.

The two criteria for choosing the topic area: 1) it is narrow or small; and 2) there is no current authority in the topic area.

It is not simply that it is better to be a big fish in a small pond than a small fish in a big pond. In the age of online programming, it is *essential* that 1) the pond be small; and 2) you are the biggest fish. Otherwise, you get eaten.

Example. You want to do a course on World War II. You are not a famous authority on World War II. Your course stands little chance of success. But you do know more than anyone else, including those famous guys, about the Battle of Strasbourg. Bingo: you are now the foremost authority in the world on the Battle of Strasbourg, now eminently qualified to teach a course on that battle and its implications on the entire war. You have an excellent chance of success with a course on the Battle of Strasbourg.

The above example about our course on World War II rests on one assumption — we want to capture a market of people interested in World War II, and we want to be known as the person with expertise on the Battle of Strasbourg.

With your teaching, the objective is not to start with you and your course and find a market. It is the exact opposite. You start with your market — the target audience — and then you build your course and expertise around the market.

In practice, you already have some kind of target audience, and you have some kind of expertise or niche with that market already. So we are linking needs and resources — your audience's needs with your resources.

We are clarifying our target market — the audience, and our niche — our area of expertise. We are becoming narrower in focus and more global in visibility.

Choose the Format

Like in-person programs, online programs will have to have the right format — time, day, length and number of sessions — in order to be successful.

With online programs, there will be even more formats from which to choose. Even more formats will be possible if your online program is combined with an in-person or on-site component.

And like the key to success with in-person and on-site programs, online program format success will be joined only by surveying your potential audience.

If the right question is asked using the proper neutral probing, your potential participants will tell you when to hold your online program, how long a session should be and how many sessions to hold.

Your participants will also tell you the best format simply by their participation in your online program. For example, if your participants have not enrolled in an online program before, they may know what topic they want and the best time of year to participate, but they may not be the best judge of how long the online program should last.

One organization was offering one-week courses online. Then they surveyed the audience whether they would like the courses to be one week, two weeks or a month in length. The vast majority said two weeks. But when the organization offered the online courses for two weeks, participation fell off dramatically in the second week, so they went back to one-week courses.

There are two lessons here. One is that your data on people's behavior is always a better indicator than what they say or think. The other lesson is that people cannot accurately gauge their interest in something they have never experienced, tried or known about before.

Summary

The key to long-term success with teaching online will be how you plan your online course. You want to position your online course to be the best there is in your particular topic area. To do that, choose your audience, choose your topic area and choose your area of expertise.

Part III.
Developing Your
Online Course

Chapter 10
Building Online Content

After you have planned your online course, including selecting your area of expertise and choosing the intended audience, you can develop your online course, seminar, training or meeting.

There are three major components of a typical online course:
1. Content
2. Interaction
3. Assessment

An online course is an educational program delivered over the Internet and having both content and interaction with participants, the interaction being either asynchronous or real time. An online course must have both components — content and interaction.

There are many self-study or tutorials, sometimes called CBT (computer-based training), programs on the Internet. This is a precursor or part of what we mean by an online course, but it does not have the interactive component necessary for the online course.

There are many online chats with authors, speakers and other experts. These experiences, while possibly very valuable, do not have an educational program content. There is not a systematic delivery of information, desired outcomes or knowledge to be acquired, nor the potential for assessment.

Let me provide another preliminary definition.

"Online seminar." An online learning experience that focuses more on the interaction between instructor and participants and among the participants themselves. There is less content provided in an online seminar than in an online course.

Building Online Content

You have chosen your subject or topic area. You have probably come up with a course title. The next step is to build your online content.

Create Modules

Divide your course or topic up into five to 10 "modules." Each module will be a separate, if interrelated, component of the course. Each module will have several knowledge skills or concepts associated with it. Each module will have a given amount of text or reading.

Illustration: Customer Service

As an illustration, if you were developing an online course in customer service, you might have these modules:

1. Why customer service is important
2. Answering the telephone
3. Dealing with complaints
4. Responding to customer interest and inquiries
5. Writing correspondence to customers
6. Doing follow up contact with customers
7. Measuring satisfaction in customer service

Modules can be sequential, beginning with the basics and then moving to more advanced information. Modules can also be entities unto themselves. That is, a module in your course could also be expanded and developed further into its own future advanced online course. Modules should lead somewhere — horizontally to the next module and/or vertically to a more intensive and advanced set of modules about the module topic area. Modules should also be able to stand-alone. That is, some of your learners will already possess the knowledge about a given module.

Develop Competencies and Outcomes

For each module, develop competencies and outcomes. These should be phrased in terms of knowledge concepts, skills, facts or figures.

This goes hand in hand with the third part of developing your online course, designing online assessment.

Select Your Readings

Next, select your readings for your online course. The readings can be both online readings and print materials.

At the time of this writing, most teachers of online courses find that print materials, such as books, magazine articles and other publications, are valuable, if not critical, material for the readings. So we would recommend you have print readings for your online course.

Within those readings, mark the pages or sections that are:

- Critical. They must be read.
- Important. They should be read.
- Nice. They could be read.

This will give your learners guidance in what you deem important. It will also give them the opportunity to pursue readings in those subject areas that are of particular interest to them. In the Information Age, the reality of the situation is that there is always more information to read than one can possibly read, no matter what the subject matter. Questions on tests should be covered in the readings that are critical for your course.

Estimate the time it takes to read the critical sections or pages in the readings. This will assist you in realistically planning how much material can be covered. And it will inform your participants how much time they should plan to devote to reading.

A rough measurement for reading time is 20 pages an hour for nonfiction, 10 pages an hour for extremely technical information, and 40 pages an hour for fiction.

If you expect your participants to spend 10 hours reading nonfiction material, then you can allocate 200 pages of reading in your critical category.

For online reading, you will want to keep the information brief. Your learners will not be able to read for long amounts of time looking at their computer screens. Also "chunk" the information. Divide it up into very small bits of information, say from one to three paragraphs per chunk.

At this time the limits of online reading all point to having your print readings be more extensive than any online readings.

Select Links to Other Sites

Tap the unlimited wealth of information on the Internet. Select links to other web sites on the Internet. Again, divide those links into categories: Critical, Important and Nice.

A new way of communicating is emerging, one that integrates pictures and words. This visual was designed by Julie Coates of LERN to encourage participants in an online discussion forum to make comments.

Think about whether you will want to write a short paragraph about each linked site, why you chose it and what the learner should look for at the site.

Make Your Online Presentations

You can make online presentations in one or more of these ways:
1. Written text.
2. Visual graphic presentation.
3. Audio
4. Video

Written text. You can write your presentations and present them as text online. If you do this, break up the copy. Divide your information into chunks.

Visual graphic presentation. Create pictures, graphs, charts and other visuals online, accompanied by either text or verbal presentation, or both. A variety of software is available to help you create good visuals. Think of the pictures as online overheads or slides. The best visuals are not merely words enlarged or put into color. The best visuals are usually true pictures or graphics.

There is a small but growing art and science of creating a new kind of visual that combines a picture with words to convey a concept better than either words or pictures could do alone. Julie Coates, Vice President of Information Services for LERN, is one pioneer in communicating in this form.

You can also incorporate text and/or audio to accompany the visuals. This is more effective than either text, visuals or audio alone. Type a paragraph or two above or below each visual explaining the visual. Or number each visual (Exhibit A, for example) and in your audio presentation, call attention to each visual as you speak about it.

Together, the audio and visual presentation is a better version of the traditional in-person lecture. In your recorded online presentation, you will be able to perfect both the content and the delivery. The learner will be able to target those portions of your presentation most relevant to their learning. They will be able to listen and view the presentation at the optimal time of the day for their learning receptivity. This will be one of the truly remarkable aspects of online learning.

Development Costs for an Online Course

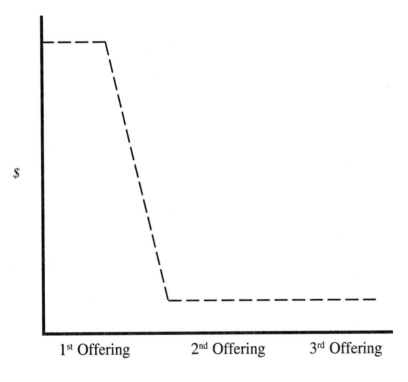

As the graph illustrates, content-rich online courses will have a high initial development cost, but very little cost after that. This is another reason why high volume, repeatable courses will be economically feasible online.

Audio Presentations

You can do either real-time oral presentations or prerecorded oral presentations. By far the more effective will be the prerecorded oral presentations. Prerecorded audio presentations have these advantages and characteristics:

- They allow you to present your best shot, both content and delivery-wise.
- You have to deliver the information only once. Thereafter, you can conserve your time and energy for interaction with your participants or developing new information and presentations.
- Your participants can listen to your presentation at their optimal time of the day.
- Your participants can review and re-listen to portions of your presentation.

After doing an audio presentation, develop a written table of contents for the presentation, much like songs on a CD. This highlights the primary concepts or points of your presentation, and it will tell the learner where in the presentation she or he can find each section of your talk. In this way, the learner can replay some portions that are more difficult or require extra attention on the part of the learner.

Illustration: Handling complaints (15 minutes total)

:00	Introduction
2:15	Hearing what the complainer has to say
3:33	Six ways to express empathy
7:48	Five steps to follow in handling the complaints
11:03	Giving the complainer options
14:17	Thanking the complainer
14:48	Closing the conversation

As with your text presentations, chunk your audio presentations. Devote 15 minutes to 30 minutes per audio presentation.

Video Presentations

At the time of this writing, the bandwidth or size of the "tube" of the Internet is not sufficiently large enough to provide high-quality video. Video is possible, however, and you may want to consider it.

Another option that is currently being practiced to a good degree is to create a separate videotape presentation and ship it to your participants. This has worked quite effectively for a number of online courses.

If, or when, you start using video presentations, be sure to approach the video presentation much differently than you have from traditional in-person lecture presentations. You will lose much if you view the Internet as just another technology for delivering your traditional lecture.

Development Time and Cost

One of the top questions teachers have about teaching online is the time and cost involved in developing the content of the online course.

If you are going to have a content-rich online course, development costs and time for the content aspect of your online course are high. It does take a good deal of time to develop content. There may be costs involved. But you only experience this development cost once per online course.

The high cost of development is why: a) you want to have as large a number of participants as possible; and b) you want to run your online course over and over again. It is also why you want to be as sure as possible that your online course will be the leading online course in your chosen niche subject or topic area.

It is uneconomical to run an online course with fewer than 30 participants. It is uneconomical to run an online course only once. And it is uneconomical to develop an online course and have it be overtaken by another online course of higher quality.

Once again, this is why you want your online course to be: first, best and largest.

Chapter 11
Creating Online Interaction

The heart and soul of your online course is not content, but interaction. This is where real learning and education takes place. It is the interplay between participants and you as teacher. And it is the interaction among the participants themselves.

It is where your course comes alive. It is where your learners get excited, the adrenaline starts to flow, eyes widen, brain cells explode with new information, lights go on, fun happens.

Only in an online course can you have people living in all corners of the globe participating at the same time. Only in an online course can you have everyone in the course talking at the same time. Only in an online course can you have so many participants you can divide up into small discussion groups based on special interest groups. This is what makes learning online so incredible.

This is also what distinguishes education from training. Training is generally a one way street, with content delivered by an instructor, and absorbed by the participant. Education is more a two-way street, with the learners contributing ideas and experience, learning from each other, and sharing.

As we noted in the chapter, "What an Online Classroom Looks Like," there are four ways to involve your participants in interaction:
1. The single-threaded asynchronous discussion forum
2. Threaded bulletin boards
3. Real time synchronous chat rooms
4. E-mail

Ideally, you want to use as many of the above devices as possible. But you also want to try to avoid a few pitfalls. Be careful not to create too much confusion for your learners in where to go and what to do.

Online learning is new for everyone right now. And secondly, whatever device you use you want it to be actively used and have the experience be successful. So, for your first online course, you might want to start with just the single-threaded asynchronous discussion forum. Once your participants are using that interactive tool sufficiently, then you can add the other devices. Or you can just jump in with several of the above interactive devices.

Discussion Forum

This will be your central meeting place on the Internet. This is where your participants will come to hear what you have to say, read your latest comments, ask questions and have a group discussion.

You can call this area whatever you want. In our online classroom, it is called "Presentation Hall," to indicate that's where the instructors will be. Another online course provider calls their central meeting place the "Class Conference."

Here you want to have a daily plan for interaction with your participants. Here are some tips and techniques in developing your interaction plan for your online course:

1. As a starting point, each module or topic area should have a time allocated when you answer questions, possibly ask your participants questions, engage in dialogue, and have a discussion. You may also want to use that time to present any new material or ideas you have since you posted the content for the course.

How long the discussion should last for each module is dependent on how long the course lasts. If you have a one-week online course, then each discussion might be for one day. If you have a 10-week online course, then each discussion might last for a week. For sure the discussion should be open around the clock, 24 hours a day. This does not mean you have to sit in front of your computer all day. But it does allow your participants to make comments anytime they wish.

When scheduling the times, check to see if the schedules of your target audience affects the discussion forum schedule. For example, if your target audience will be taking the online course while at work, schedule your discussion forums to take place during the day.

You will probably find that more discussion takes place on Tuesdays, Wednesdays and Thursdays. On Monday everyone is engaged in beginning the work week, and on Friday, everyone is winding up the week. For our discussion forums, for example, we don't even schedule them on Mondays or Fridays anymore, we just use Tuesday-Thursday as the schedule.

On the other hand, if your target audience will be participating from home and in their own personal time, you will want your discussion forums to take place at night and on the weekends.

2. Open discussion versus topical discussion. One of the common questions about designing a discussion forum schedule is whether to have times for "open discussion" or whether to have specific topics designated for each discussion. This is an excellent question, and at this time, there is no universally acceptable answer. So it is up to you to experiment, test, see what your participants want, or what fits with your course material. Sometimes you may want to have an "Open Discussion" where there is no specific topic to be addressed, and people can talk about anything. At other times, you will want to have the discussion focussed on a given topic.

3. Prepare for your online discussions. They won't just happen. There will not be a spontaneous outpouring of great insightful comments and questions from your participants. Initially, there will be "dead air" as they say in the broadcasting business. So you will want to create the discussion, get it started and give it momentum.

We discuss this further in-depth in the chapter "Teaching Your Online Course," but here are a few tips related to planning your online discussion.

- Do one to four comments at the beginning of each discussion. Prepare them in advance.
- Try to line up participants or guest commentators to make initial comments or questions early on in the discussion to get the ball rolling.
- Inform your participants of the upcoming discussion with an e-mail. A daily e-mail to them is a great idea.

4. Think about a secondary discussion area. Consider a second discussion area for your participants. Again, this might be too much to handle and too much to ask for your first or second online course.

But after you have taught online for awhile, you may very well see the advantage in having a second asynchronous discussion forum.

On our site, we use the second discussion forum for "learners only." The instructors stay out of it, except to ask questions at the beginning of each day. This gives the class participants an opportunity to say anything they want, ask anything or respond to other participants without having the presence of the all-knowing, authoritative, and sometimes intimidating, instructor there to correct or comment.

Someone is constructing our Web Page and I am to keep it updated once it is in place. Thanks again.

From: Marilane Bond (mbond@medadm.emory.edu) Tue Nov 11 13:59:11 EST 1997

Good Afternoon! Marilane Bond from Continuing Medical Education at Emory University in Atlanta, Ga.

From: Sharon Thomas (sharon@hondros.com) Tue Nov 11 14:04:32 EST 1997

As I am someone who learns best by example (particularly, not to repeat bad examples), the Web Pages that Suck site was very helpful! Thanks!

From: Patty Hoerner (phoerner@ccmail.llu.edu) Tue Nov 11 14:11:36 EST 1997

Hello Everyone. I have attended two other presentations given by Lenny Charnoff and have learned immense amounts regarding our web site for continuing dental education. We too are unable to register online at this time. However, I have received our registration form printed out and mailed or faxed to me.

From: lenny charnoff (charnoff@netogether.com) Tue Nov 11 14:13:15 EST 1997

Tnx for the comments on Web Pages That Suck. Go to it :-) Don't worry your web site won't be on it. Another great site is <u>Cool Tool</u> I usually don't recommend sites that are "cool" but this site has a great business model as well as "unorthodox" approaches to life. They also have a collection of web editing tools to look at. It's also a great example of "superb web site"

From: lenny charnoff (charnoff@netogether.com) Tue Nov 11 14:19:46 EST 1997

Brochure On The Web. Great idea. Two caveats. 1. The Web is not print. Be careful that you redesign it for speed, graphics and horizontal format 2. Your brochure on the web should be interactive with plenty of places for your viewer to leave their e-mail address. I have been here since 7:00am pst. One of the great parts about working at home and on the Net is that you get a chance to do things you really like. I'm taking Snulla, my Icelandic mare, for a short ride. Will be back by 1:30pm. Please e-mail me anything and the answer will be in your e-mail tomorrow morning

From: Greg Marshall (computergy@memes.com) Tue Nov 11 14:21:31 EST 1997

Web Tools: Lets not forget Netscape. I use Netscape to create webpages and find it really easier to use and not as proprietary as Frontpage. I also use Office 97 to convert documents, spreadsheets and such into html and then use Netscape to finish the project.

From: Greg Ledford (gledford@mayland.cc.nc.us) Tue Nov 11 14:31:39 EST 1997

Re: Greg Marshall 14:21:31 I agree. My team finds Netscape easier to work with for creating and applying finishing touches. The trick here seems to be Office 97. Tell me...is this really the best way of porting to html?

This is what a discussion forum looks like.

You may also want to use a threaded bulletin board instead as a secondary mechanism to get input and feedback from your participants.

5. Consider scheduling one or more real-time discussion forums. Your basic and fundamental interactive mechanism should be the asynchronous discussion forum that is open 24 hours a day. But as a supplement, some instructors have found it useful to add a specific time of the day when the instructor is at the computer and the answers or comments are posted almost immediately.

For example, Julie Coates scheduled a one-hour period during the day and told her online class participants she would be there — no waiting for a reply. She scheduled it for 2-3 p.m. Eastern Time in the United States. It proved so successful she actually stayed online for two hours, answering all the questions that came in.

This technique is going to be more successful for online classes with larger numbers of participants, say 50 and above. It is not going to be as successful for online classes with 30 or fewer participants.

6. Saving and archiving the discussions. One very positive and useful aspect of the asynchronous discussion forum is the ability to save and archive the discussion. By saving and archiving the discussion, your participants can view and download the comments at any time in the future, as long as you want them to have access to it.

You should plan on making arrangements with your webmaster or technical assistance person to routinely and regularly save and archive the discussions. For a relatively active discussion, saving and archiving the discussion on a daily basis is advisable.

You should also save and archive the discussions to disk and also keep a hard copy or printout for future reference. This will be a valuable source of material for future online courses, reference, information, and research.

Threaded Bulletin Boards

Threaded bulletin boards are wonderful tools with many uses. However, you should not use a threaded bulletin board as your central discussion forum. Use the asynchronous single-threaded discussion forum for that. Threaded bulletin boards are especially useful for posting static or stand-alone comments. Here are some things you can do with threaded bulletin boards:

1. Message or comment board. If you want your participants to make comments on a number of different topics, a threaded bulletin

○ Exit   ○ New   Messages   ○ Search   ○ Options   ○ Logout/in   ○ Users   ○ Messages

Active threads from last 365 days:

○ New Thread   ○ Refresh

▼ STUDENT COMMENTS

○ June	10/30/98	(2)
○ Chuck	09/22/98	(3)
○ Ralph	09/22/98	(6)
○ Betty	09/16/98	(3)
○ Susan	08/20/98	(2)
○ Bill	06/03/98	(2)
○ August	05/28/98	(1)
○ Sherri	05/28/98	(1)
○ May	05/28/98	(1)
○ April	05/28/98	(1)
○ Bob	05/28/98	(1)
○ Chuck T.	05/28/98	(1)

▲ SUB TOPICS (16)

▲ REFERENCES (5)

○ **Subscribe to Thread**

This is what a threaded bulletin board looks like.

board is a good way to go. Each thread would be a different topic, and your participants would post their comments on the appropriate thread.

2. An individual record. If you want each of your participants to post information, homework or comments, you could set up a threaded bulletin board. Each thread would be the name of a different person in your class, and the person would post her or his comments in his or her own thread.

3. Daily question. Every day, you could ask a different question and have all your participants respond. Each thread would then be a separate date, along with the question of the day.

4. Directories, references and much more. There are a thousand other uses for threaded bulletin boards. They are used as directories of individuals. They are used to store references to other information, books and links. They are used as an online "classified ads" section, with people buying and selling products or just posting ideas. Use a threaded bulletin board if it is useful for you.

Real-Time Chat Rooms

A real-time chat room, sometimes called an IRC (Internet Relay Chat), is synchronous or "live." Venture into this online chat device at your own risk. If you want to use this device, you set up a time for a chat and invite or encourage all your participants to get online at the same time.

There are two challenges with real-time chat rooms for online classes:

1. <u>Time differences</u>. If your participants are all in the same time zone, then there is no problem. But more and more online courses will want and benefit from having participants in many different time zones, and thus scheduling a time when everyone is awake, much less available, becomes difficult.

2. <u>Short comments</u>. A real-time chat room has the capability for only short comments. Longer comments do not work well in a real-time chat room because of the time it takes to post them, and because comments scroll up and out of view so very quickly.

Real-time chat rooms may have a place in your online course. But again, there is the problem of trying to get everyone on at the same time, possibly dealing with different time zones.

And the real educational challenge is to try to get anything but a chatty "how are you" discussion going with substantive comments and thoughts. The screen just rolls up too quickly for many people to be able to pose a thoughtful remark.

Live Chat (IRC)

Carl: Hi, welcome.
Sherry: Thanks, good to be here.
Carl: What's up?
Sherry: Nothing much. How are you?
Carl: I'm great.
Carl: So, what's the biggest issue for you and your organization?
Sherry: Well, that's a big question. Let me start by saying that...

This is what a live chat room looks like.

E-mail

E-mail is a wonderful tool. And it has many uses. Use e-mail to:

- Contact everyone in the course at various times, update them on changes in the course, or simply encourage them to participate online.
- For strictly individual-to-individual comments, including dealing with a learner's problems, e-mail is the only way to go.
- Use e-mail autoresponders to send information out to prospective participants for an upcoming course.
- E-mail test scores or evaluative comments to your participants.

E-mail should not be used as the central discussion or dialogue mode of communication. This does not allow others to participate or benefit from learner questions, comments and sharing. But for many other communication issues, e-mail is a great tool.

Chapter 12
Designing Online Assessment

The third major component of an online course is, or can be, assessment. Assessments are most often thought of as tests and quizzes, but on the Internet the whole nature of tests and quizzes changes, enhancing learning and contributing positively to the learning experience. Doing assessments is not necessary for an online course. But it is such a valuable tool for learners, so easy to implement and full of so much potential that doing assessments for your online course will be a great addition to your teaching.

Before we discuss ways to design and implement assessments, we need to talk a little about how outcomes, measurements and evaluations of learning experiences will change in the Information Age and online.

In the Industrial Age, the 20th century, a major part of assessment was based on attendance, just being there. As Woody Allen is purported to have said, "90 percent of success is just showing up." Many measurements of education are based on attendance. For example, take continuing education units, or CEUs, one measurement of continuing education for adults. A CEU is earned by attending an educational program of 10 hours.

But online, attendance is both difficult to measure and irrelevant. It is not difficult to measure the number of times a person logs on to your course. But what the person is doing while logging on is much harder to determine.

New technologies may solve the problem of measuring participation. But the bigger issue is that attendance or putting in one's time is now irrelevant. What matters now is outcomes and results — whether you or I have actually learned something. It matters much less how much time we put into the effort. You may learn Module A in half the time I do, and I may learn Module B in half the time you do. Every person putting the same amount of time into the same subject matter, regardless of the learner's previous experience, aptitude for that subject, or ability to learn, no longer makes sense.

And so we are moving toward outcomes and results as a measure of learning. If you pass the test, you know the stuff. It doesn't matter how much time you put in, or how many times you logged on, if you pass it, you know it. And if you don't pass the test, you don't know it.

This change in desired outcomes in learning from attendance to results is causing a change in the way we do tests and evaluations as well. We are moving away from more subjective evaluations, more generalized or sampling questions. We are moving toward more core questions, toward more multiple choice tests, more questions dealing with the central ideas and skills of the course.

What this means is that online, both teacher and learner can reap enormous benefits from the new possibilities of doing assessments. Here are three different kinds of assessments to consider for your online course.

Pre-Course Assessment

Use a pre-course assessment in two ways: First, to help prospective participants determine whether your online course is right for them; and second, to determine the level of knowledge of each of your participants before they begin your course.

Here's how to do it. Create a 10-question multiple choice quiz. Ten questions is enough to get a good sense of the knowledge of the person, but short enough that most people won't be deterred from taking the quiz. The questions should be ones that people will be able to answer at the end of your course. In fact, they could even be the questions from your final exam, assuming you have a final exam.

For prospective participants determining whether your online course is right for them, the pre-course assessment is helpful in several ways:

1. It tells them about the content of your course and what they will learn. The questions on your quiz will reflect what they can expect to learn. If this is not the subject matter they were hoping for, it is better for them, and you, that they not enroll. So this information is helpful to them.
2. It tells them how much they already know. If, for some reason, they know all the material already, then they may not need the course. This rarely happens. What most always happens is that

people do poorly on the pre-course assessment, and the quiz helps show them how much they will learn by taking your course.

3. The quiz establishes a benchmark for both you as a teacher and the individual learner. By measuring how well a person does before taking your course, you are now able to measure progress and demonstrate how much they gained from the course by comparing their pre-course score with their final evaluation score.

4. Another benefit is that you as instructor have a good idea what your participants know, and don't know, as they come to your course. This helps you emphasize certain content areas, spend less time on the things they already know, and in general teach them better.

The results of the pre-course assessment should be made available immediately to the person taking the quiz. And the results should be stored so that you as teacher can have access to them to assist you in preparing your course and in benchmarking the person's pre and post course scores. No one else need know the quiz scores.

Progress Assessments

A terrific new opportunity for learning now exists online in helping your participants measure their progress on a weekly or even daily basis. While it is possible that some teachers may have given weekly or daily tests using paper and pencil, it has not been common nor easy. Now it is so easy that progress assessments will be a great learning and teaching tool.

Once again, you devise a 10-question multiple choice quiz. Once again, it does not have to be exactly 10 questions. You post the quizzes in your online classroom. There are several technical software programs to make this quite easy to do.

One way is to have the person check the answers on the screen, submit the quiz after she or he is done, and then immediately be given a screen with all the correct answers.

Another way is to have the quiz be in the form of an e-mail. The e-mail is sent to an autoresponder, and the autoresponder immediately sends back the correct answers.

For my first quizzes, I had participants e-mail me their answers and then I e-mailed back the answers and a few encouraging comments.

And there are other software programs available to assist in this as well.

The correct answers are immediately given back to the participant, so she or he knows how well she has done. The person can then review some material he missed, or move ahead if the scores look pretty good.

You as an instructor then have the option of getting the progress assessment scores, or not. If they are helpful to you and if you have the time, you can review them and adjust your teaching. If you have a large number of participants in your online course, or more limited time, you don't have to review the scores.

If you are interested in monitoring the progress of each participant more closely, the progress assessment quizzes will help you do that. If a person scores low on a series of quizzes, then you and that person know there is some special effort that has to be made. If a person does not even take the quiz, then you know something as well.

Progress assessment quizzes are a great learning tool. They will speed up the learning. They will refocus the learning around the areas that need attention for a particular learner. And they will inform you as teacher how well folks are doing, and whether you need to be more advanced, back up, repeat some material or move more quickly in your instruction.

End-of-Course Tests

The third use of an assessment is to evaluate how much the person has learned by the end of your course.

Once again, we recommend a multiple choice test for most online courses dealing with cognitive knowledge. If you want to do an essay exam, that is up to you. If you are doing a course for which a formal evaluation is not necessary, think about doing an optional quiz for the benefit of your learners. These quizzes really do help people learn.

Your end-of-course test should be entirely composed of questions related to the central, core, essential and critical knowledge skills of your course. They may be the same questions as are on your pre-course assessment. There is nothing wrong with saying, "These are things I will teach, these are the things you should know."

Another one of the most popular questions about online teaching is how to tell if the person taking the online test is really the person who registered for the course. New technology will solve this problem shortly.

But for now, the best advice is not to worry about it. If it happens, then you can devote some of your valuable time and energy to fixing the problem. The truth is that very few people will risk their careers and good name for the sake of cheating in an online course. And the truth is also that a few people have been cheating in courses for centuries and will continue to do so without impacting on the validity or reputation of the course, teacher or sponsoring organization.

Now, if you do want to devote some of your valuable time and energy trying to combat the possibility that someone may be cheating on an online exam, here are some things to do:

- Develop daily quizzes. It will cost the cheating individual a lot of money to pay for someone to take a quiz every day. Make sure you check the routing of the e-mail so that you can determine if it comes from the computer or ISP of the individual in your class.
- If someone is not doing well on the daily quizzes, but aces the final test, check that person out.
- Call a suspected individual and just ask her or him the same question they answered correctly in a recent quiz or test.
- Have proctors for your final online test. It is even more unlikely that two people will risk their careers and good names.

But once again, this is not a widespread problem at this point in online learning. It is only a widespread perceived problem.

Steps in Developing Your Online Course

1. Divide up your content matter into five to 10 discrete modules.
2. Select readings that are Critical, Important and Nice to Read.
3. Create a set of objectives for your online course.
4. Create a set of questions that you want each participant to know. The answers to the questions must be found in your Critical readings and/or contained in your presentations.
5. Write the quizzes and tests for the course.
6. Create a pre-course assessment quiz.
7. Develop a plan for delivering the content of the online course.
8. Create a plan and time schedule for the interaction among participants and yourself.

You can spend a little time developing your online course, or a lot. While normally we recommend as much preparation for a course as possible, the situation with online learning right now is a little different. There is much to be explored, there is much to be learned, about teaching online. So don't agonize too long over your online course. Do what you can, then jump into it. You will probably learn a whole lot more by teaching your first online course than you will by guessing what will or might happen in advance of your course.

Part IV.
Teaching Your
Online Course

Chapter 13
Teaching Your Online Course

Constructing an Agenda

A week or so before the beginning of your course, your participants should have an agenda. The agenda should tell them:

1. What technical requirements or software they need in order to participate in your course.
2. The course goals and objectives.
3. An outline of the content — topics or modules — included in your course. After each topic, you will want to include the readings, audio, links and other content available pertaining to that topic or module.
4. The schedule for interaction, dialogue, discussion forums or chats.
5. The pre-assessment quiz, or instructions on completing it, if you have one.
6. Rules or guidelines for participating in the course. This might include:
   - Expectations, such as the number of times a person should get online, or noting that participants are expected to make comments during the discussions or chats.
   - Procedures, such as how and when to e-mail the instructor, what format a paper is to be submitted, or how and when to communicate with other participants.
   - Ethics, such as using your real name rather than a made up name online, not presenting other's work as your own, or not getting help or assistance on the tests.
7. Participants list. The list can be basic, including name, address and so on. Or you could enhance the participants list in a variety

of ways to encourage people to get to know one another and interact in and outside of your online course. You could:

- Provide e-mail addresses so participants can communicate with each other.
- Have a short biography. Each participant could write one paragraph, which you post on your site, about her or himself. It could be biographical, or it could be about their interest and experience in the subject matter of your course.
- Picture. You could post a picture of each participant, or have a link to another site where their picture is posted.
- Web site link. Many people have their own web site, or are part of organizations with web sites, and you could provide the URL to your participants' web sites.

8. Where to go and pre-course activities. You should tell participants how to get into your online course. And you might want to have them test your site out a day or two before the course starts to make sure they are comfortable with navigating your site.

9. Problems or questions. Always have some address, place or person to get in touch with in case a participant has a problem or question. It could be your e-mail address. It could be your webmaster's e-mail or phone number. It could be a toll-free phone number. Reassure your participants by giving them a contact in case they encounter a problem or question.

The agenda, along with a nice welcome from you as instructor, should be sent to participants. It could go out at the time they register for your course. It could be sent a week before. You could mail it or e-mail it.

Welcoming Your Participants

It may only be two or three sentences. It may only take three minutes. But it is very important that you welcome your participants. Tell them you are glad they are participating. Reinforce that they will get something valuable out of the course. Express your pleasure at the quantity or quality of the participants who are involved. Convey your excitement about them contributing to the course. Reassure them. It is very important you set the stage before you begin your course. As Jerry Apps once said, "Make them believe." A few ways to break the ice online:

- In the first minute of the first hour of the course, type in your discussion forum or chat room a short, one-paragraph comment welcoming people to your course.

- Invite all participants to simply type their name and indicate they are logged on that day.
- Invite all participants to make a short statement about who they are, why they came, or their previous experience in the subject area. Make it an easy task, something people do not have to think too much about, and something that tells a little something about each one as a person.
- Tell people if they are having problems or questions to contact you immediately.

However you do it, welcome people to your course. It will put them in a positive frame of mind about their involvement in your course.

The First Day

The first day of your online course is the most important day of the course, regardless how long your online course will be. If the first day goes well, you are off to a good start. If the first day goes poorly, you have damage control to do, and some courses never fully recover from a bad first day. If something goes wrong on the fifth day, they will forgive you. But if something goes wrong on the first day, their enthusiasm will be dimmed, they will expect further things to go wrong, they will begin to question whether they made a good choice.

Here are things to think about to make your first day online go well:

- Technical back up. The Internet goes down. Wires get overloaded. Computers get glitches. Things happen. Do whatever you can to ensure that things go technically well the first day. You should be at a computer with good connections. Try not to be traveling, on the road or working from a hotel on the first day. Get your technical person to be "on alert" and immediately available on that first day.
- Solve problems. As best you can, find out if any of your participants are having problems. The problems usually come early on in your course. If someone has a problem the first day and it is not fixed until later, it will have seriously negative influence on that person's learning, participation and satisfaction with the course. So anything you can do to find out about problems, and then address them, is positive. Even if it is a technical problem with the person's own computer and totally out of your control, your response or understanding will be helpful to that person.
- Recap the goals or objectives. Begin by telling people what will happen in the course. Do this in a summary fashion. The complete

goals and objectives and schedule will be in your agenda. But rephrase what will happen, make it pointed and forceful and positive. This will help people focus or refocus.

- Invite interaction immediately. As soon as you can, invite your participants to participate and contribute. Whether it is just putting in their name or filling out a quick survey or question form — the sooner they are involved physically (typing, making a comment), the sooner they are involved emotionally and motivationally.
- Give 'em your best stuff. We have a rule of thumb for people attending conference sessions. If the session is not good in the first five or 10 minutes, get up and walk out to another session, because that session is not going to get any better. You want to make a good first impression with your online course. The way to do that is to start off strong.

Here are some tips for starting off strong.

- Jump right into the content. The best way to start off strong is to get right into the content. Give them something to chew on immediately. Too many courses dilly dally around, talking about what people "will" learn in the rest of the course, without getting right to the matter at hand. Spend as little time as possible on the formalities, guidelines and so on. Jump right into your content.
- Give them your best stuff. Your first module, content or day online should be as strong or stronger than the rest of the course. If you can make a good impression on the first day, you've got them. If you don't, you could lose them.

If you can bring out some of your best points, or a sample of the good stuff, that will get people excited. At a minimum, make the quality of your first day's content the same level as the rest of the course. And if you can add a little extra something that first day, do it.

- Begin your dialogue. Get into your discussion forum or chat room. Make a few comments. Get things going.
- The more planning, the better. The more planning, even rehearsing of the first day, the better. You don't need to rehearse or plan details for the rest of the course. But the first day of your online course is so important that it is worth writing out in advance your online comments, preparing a little bit more, doing a little bit more, for that first day.

Make that first day good, and you will be going downhill from there. If that first day doesn't go well, it will be uphill the rest of the course. The first day is important. Make it a good one.

Delivering Content

As we noted earlier, you have a number of choices in delivering content to your online course participants. You can choose:
- Readings, such as books, publications, articles
- Online readings
- Links to other sites and information on the web
- Live audio on the Internet
- Recorded audio on the Internet
- Audio cassettes or CDs mailed to participants
- CD-ROMs
- Video on the Internet
- Videos mailed to the participants
- Visuals and graphics, with or without commentary, with or without audio
- Discussion forums and chat rooms

Use the content formats that make sense for you. We do know that the more variety in the way information is delivered, the more effective the learning. Some learners learn best orally, some visually, some with text, some by demonstration or hands-on discovery. So if you have the opportunity to deliver content in more than one medium or format, do so. Your participants will benefit. Regardless of the ways you deliver your content, you should:
- Repeat the content schedule. Reiterate with your participants as they go through your course what content they should be reading or listening or viewing at each stage of the course.
- Summarize in your discussion forum or chat room the highlights or most important points in the content matter.

Making Content Comments

It will be very helpful for you to make content comments in your discussion forum or chat room. The content comments from you help to tie things together and create a flow with your online course. They also tell your participants what information you value highly and what aspects of the subject matter they should explore fully.

Here are some tips on making content comments in your discussion forum or chat room:
- <u>Make your comments short</u>. From six to eight lines of copy is a good rule of thumb.

- <u>Just do one thought per comment</u>. Don't try to string together more than one thought, concept or idea in a comment. Focus each comment on just one thought.
- <u>Use highlighting techniques</u>. Feel free to underline some of your copy, boldface a few words, create a headline or otherwise highlight parts of your comments.
- <u>Don't think online</u>. Don't try to do too much thinking online while writing your comments. Composing a well-constructed paragraph of comment takes some forethought, and you should have a good idea what you want to say when you write it.
- <u>Feel free to do a draft</u>. Sometimes I type a comment in my typewriter and revise it before entering it online. Feel free to do a draft of your comments.
- <u>Focus on important issues</u>. Keep your comments oriented toward the important concepts or ideas in your course. Obviously you could go on and talk about a lot of issues online, but time and space is limited, so focus your comments on the most important ideas you want to convey.
- <u>Be careful about humor</u>. It is much harder to express humor online. Be very open about humor. For example, "This is a joke..." Trying to be subtle with humor online will only confuse some of your participants.
- <u>Present new info</u>. If you have new or current information not contained in your prepared content or readings, using the discussion forum or chat room is a good way to deliver that recent or new information.

Stimulating Interaction

To repeat, interaction online is the heart and guts of your online course. This is where all the excitement takes place. This is where the real learning happens. This is where the Internet is vastly superior to in-person learning. This is how an online course differs from a self tutorial.

As an online teacher, you will be making two kinds of comments in your discussion forum or chat room: 1) content comments; and 2) discussion comments. It is important you understand that discussion comments differ in style and substance from content comments. Content comments are meant to deliver information. Discussion comments are meant to encourage your participants to interact. Here are some tips on moderating a discussion online:

- View the discussion as a conversation, a dialogue. You are a moderator or discussion facilitator. Keep the comments coming. Encourage people to interact.
- Get one or two people to make some initial comments or questions. If you just "open it up" to questions, you will see a blank screen for an awfully long time. Instead, arrange ahead of time for one or more participants to enter a comment or question to get the discussion going. Once you get two to four comments in there, you have a discussion going.
- When getting a question, first compliment the person on the question. Tell her or him, "Thanks for asking;" "Good question;" "Glad you asked that." Encourage people to ask questions. It is difficult to ask a question online — the person has to compose the question carefully and thoughtfully and has to feel confident enough to post it.
- Allow others to respond to questions and make comments. Don't shut off discussion by making too authoritative a comment.
- Make sure someone responds to every comment. Every time someone makes a comment online, someone else should respond to it. Don't let thoughts or comments dangle unresponded.
- Look for connections. Try to connect several of your participants' comments or questions, citing similarities or differences among them. This creates a conversation, helps the line of thinking and helps your participants put together a more cohesive reading of the discussion.

Moderating a discussion online is one of the key and critical skills you will want to develop as an online teacher. Online, as in person, you will want to "listen" to your participants. Here are some tips:

- Look to create "door openers." When someone makes an initial comment online, ask if they would like to follow up with more information. "Tell me more" is one way to put it. Or you can ask a follow-up question.
- Be neutral and nonjudgmental. Russell Robinson, in *Helping Adults Learn and Change*, makes some good points we can adapt to the online learning situation:
  - Try to understand what is meant when the person makes a comment.
  - Don't try to contradict or refute a person's ideas too quickly.
  - Put aside your own views when responding to others.
  - Expect the participant's language to be different from your own.
  - Avoid negative feedback.
- Help insecure learners. Learners who lack self confidence are common in adult learning. A good teacher needs to make the learning

environment secure for these people. Building their confidence is not condescending, instead it keeps their desire to learn alive.

- Offer rewards. Look for ways to offer rewards to your participants. The reward could be a positive comment. It could be an information "gift," such as a reference to a new link or site. Or it could be a physical gift, such as a free report or article mailed to the person. Rewards are positive reinforcements for the person and for everyone else in class as well.
- Have expectations of your participants. Australian Philip C. Candy, in his book *Self Direction for Lifelong Learning,* has this to say about enhancing security: "Educators who hold high expectations for their students tend to convey these through complex and subtle patterns of interaction, which commonly result in the learners living up to these expectations, and in the process, developing a more positive image of themselves."
- Help with frustration. Sometimes learners will demean themselves, professing inadequacy, frustration or outside interference. When the learner is unhappy about some situation, focus on how the student feels about the external situation, not the situation itself. When someone expresses frustration or inadequacy, you should do the following:
  - Don't contradict the person's views.
  - Don't use logical explanations.
  - Don't ridicule the person's view.
  - Do convey your positive regard for the person.
- Encourage shy participants. Some participants prefer to be quiet and "lurk" and learn that way. Privacy deserves respect, but there are some overtures you as the teacher can make without intruding. Patience, invitations to make comments, and other strategies, like devising group exercises that involve making comments, can involve quiet learners without embarrassing them.
- Avoid negative reinforcement. Some of your participants will do or say things that are wrong. When someone does something wrong, don't punish that person by calling attention to the wrong comment or embarrassing the person. This is punishment and it is counterproductive. Punishment has inhibited more learning in a person's lifetime, and indeed throughout history, than any other single factor. Instead, use positive encouragement.
- Steps in positive teaching. In *Yes, You Can Teach,* Florence Nelson outlines the four steps of encouragement to maintain the learning

climate throughout the class. Encouragement is not always effusive praise. Providing encouragement can be a subtle art, and it is a changing process depending on the needs of the learner. Nelson points to a four-step process that helps the learner become self-directed while lessening the role of the teacher. It illustrates that the best teachers are those who can step aside when the learner is ready. These are the four steps of encouragement:

1. The fundamentals. In the beginning, effusive praise like "great," "wonderful," "Keep it going."
2. Pleasing you the teacher. As they advance, let them know, "it is coming along well," "Now you've got the right idea," and so on.
3. Pleasing you and themselves. Still further along, encourage them with comments like "Yes, that's it...how do you feel about it?" or "I can see some progress here, what do you think?" or "I'll bet you're proud of yourself."
4. Pleasing themselves. And finally, when the learner is well along, you can say, "When you need help, just let me know."

Chapter 14
Promoting Your Online Course

One of the earliest misconceptions about marketing on the Internet was that all you had to do was put your program on your web site, and maybe other web sites, and presto, registrations and business would come flowing in.

Far from devoting fewer resources to promotion and marketing, successful online programs will devote more resources to promotion and marketing. More marketing, in fact, not less, will be necessary in the 21st century.

That being said, however, we cannot emphasize enough the reality that increased promotion, even terrific quality promotion, cannot save or rescue a program that does not meet the perceived needs of the audience. You simply have to have the right program — as defined by your audience.

If you do have the right program, it will not sell itself, of course. But you will find it much easier, and spend your promotion dollars more efficiently and effectively if you are promoting the "right program."

So promotion will follow program development. And be prepared to do more promotion, not less, over the long run.

OK, But Not Enough

Here are some promotional things that are commonly mistaken to be great promotional techniques. They are OK to do — nothing hurts — but they are not sufficient to promote your online course. If you do them, do them as tests, as adjuncts or supplements, but do not expect results. They don't work, at least not yet.

1. Listing your program on master web sites.
2. Listing your program on other organizations' web sites.
3. Unsolicited e-mail. E-mail users can receive dozens of junk mail solicitations a day, but they do not like junk e-mail messages.
4. Rented e-mail lists. A few e-mail lists exist that you can rent, but most likely you will be wasting your money on them.
5. Listing your program on your own web site. You should list your online program on your web site. And you should provide complete — or more than complete — information about your online program on your web site. But your web site will be a follow-up to traditional direct mail promotion. Your web site alone won't sell your programs.

Of course, you should continue to develop and build your web site to make it as accessible, attractive and income producing as possible. That includes taking registrations on your web site.

What Does Work

Direct Mail
What works today is to develop a traditional brochure and mail it out at least once to your targeted audience.

This medium will bring in the bulk of your registrations for one simple reason. People are used to it. People are familiar with it. People find out about in-person or on-site programs through direct mail and register for them.

Brochures
Brochures promoting online programs need to use the A.I.D.A. (Attract, Interest, Desire, Action) approach and follow all the rules of success for program brochures.

In addition, consider these additional points:
1. Whenever possible, use visuals and graphics that are computer-age. Your audience is by qualification technology literate and attuned to computer graphics. Using computer-age visuals and graphics sends the right message that your organization understands technology, and that you're practicing what you preach.
2. Your brochure may be shorter in length. This has not been tested, but we suspect you can produce a shorter brochure for online programs. With in-person or on-site programs, higher quality and higher cost programs have often benefitted from longer brochures

to project that quality in image. However, in promoting online programs, participants are not likely to need long brochures for one perceptual reason: They will expect complete information on the program to be available on your web site.

3. Online benefits. Be sure to include benefits of taking the program online versus taking it in person. For example, you could stress that participants can be involved anytime day or night, there are no time restrictions. Or that you have more presenters than available for an on-site program. Or that they can network with participants all over the world.

4. Relate the technology necessary. Tell people how they will log on, what hardware or software is required, and briefly state how they will participate technologically in the program. Do not be too elaborate. Provide only enough information to attract interest. Send details and specifics with confirmation or explain it further on your web site, not in your brochure.

5. Reference, but don't require, a visit to your web site. Tell people there is more information on your web site. They will expect that. But don't require a visit to your web site to get any vital information — such as agenda, instructors, price. People should be able to have all the info they need in the brochure in order to be able to make a decision and register.

6. Accept traditional ways of registration. Online registration is happening and will grow. Someday, maybe soon, almost all of your registration will come off your web site. But not now. Be sure to include a traditional registration form in your brochure, and invite people to register via mail, fax and phone as well as by e-mail and on your web site.

To Whom Should You Mail?

Mail to best prospects, to your past participants. Your best customers for your online programs are likely to have the same demographic characteristics and be the same people who are your best customers for your on-site programs.

With one exception. You now have the opportunity to go global, so do it. For in-person or on-site programs you mail to the surrounding geographical region. But for online programs you can and should begin to mail much more broadly, nationally or even internationally.

The place to start is with any names currently in your mailing list from outside your current service area. Next, begin to strategize low-cost ways of obtaining addresses of people who look just like your best participants demographically speaking.

At the time of this writing, gathering a global mailing list is still a cutting edge idea. In a few years it will become a necessity in order to maximize income and registrations. And shortly thereafter the global mailing list (it may be an e-mail list by then) will become critical. That is, if you have the list you can dominate your niche and be the global winner for your particular online program. And, without the global list, you will be far behind the winner or maybe not able to be a player at all. So right now you may not want to dump thousands of dollars into finding international customers. But you do want to start right now thinking globally. And every international name you can acquire in a low-cost manner is golden. Mail to any international names you have.

Another important aspect of whom you should mail to is to not explore a totally new audience. In general, if you explore an audience that does not demographically resemble your current audience, you are playing a high-risk game. And online programs for the next few years will be high enough risk as we find out what works and what doesn't — we don't need any more risks.

There may be some of you who discover a huge untapped and ready market for online programs. If you can design a product line around your newly found untapped market, go for it.

But most of us will want to stay with our current strengths and build on our best customers.

Here are two illustrations of what I am talking about.

Example 1. You currently offer a program of courses for electrical engineers. You develop an online program. You find a mailing list of electrical engineers in Finland, along with the fact that Finns have a high rate of access to the Internet (which they do).

Yes, you should definitely mail to the Finnish electrical engineers (all other things being equal).

Example 2. You currently offer a program of courses for nurses. You find a large mailing list of Finnish electrical engineers, along with the fact that they all have access to the Internet. No, you should not try to promote to Finnish electrical engineers, or American ones either — it's not your market niche.

How Many to Mail

This is a very good question and there is currently little data on how many brochures to mail for an online program. So here's what to do.

1. Mail the same number of brochures as you would for an in-person or on-site program. Add to this number any international names you have. Now you can compare your response rate with existing programs.
2. Budget your online program to break even in the beginning and allocate 25 percent of income for promotion. This will give you your best shot. You are not spending too little on promotion at 25 percent. And your objective is to get your online programs working. Later you can increase your operating or profit margin.

One organization mailed 4,000 brochures to its best customers, including international. Normally, the organization mailed 6,000 brochures to 3,000 people (averaging two brochures per person) to a specific geographical region for an on-site seminar. The one-time mailing was expected to generate 50 registrations for the online seminar. Instead it generated 300 registrations, so promotion was less than 10 percent of income.

So you can achieve immediate success, a high number of registrations, and low promotion costs. But do not expect such immediate results. This is a long-term game, and the immediate objective is to capture the online market. If you do, you will then be able to capture the online dollars.

When to Mail

Mail at the same time as you would for an on-site program. This is 14 weeks out for most successful seminars and continuing professional education programs. Allowing two weeks for bulk mail, people will get the brochure three months out.

Currently there is no evidence that people expect an online program brochure any earlier, or any later, than an on-site program brochure. And there is no evidence people make the decision to attend an online program any later than they would for an on-site program, even though an online program involves no travel, hotel or canceled meetings.

There is evidence to suggest that people register right up until the first day of an online program. In fact, some people register after the online program has started and read the transcripts to catch up.

But the registration pattern does not necessarily mean the time of deciding to register has changed.

At this point it is safest to assume that most people still make their decision to attend one to two months out, accustomed as they are to this time frame for their on-site program commitments. That may very well change as online programs become more common, but there is no reason to believe at this point that mailings less than 14 weeks before the online program starts will be any more effective. So mail 14 weeks out.

What Will Work Next: From Mail to E-mail

We will probably always have brochures and mailing lists. Our experience with technology is that new technologies don't replace old ones — they just add to them. Fax registration did not replace phone registration, it just added to it. E-mail registration will not replace fax or phone registration, just add to it.

But the nature and function of brochures and mailing lists are likely to change. Right now your brochure and mailings are everything, or almost everything, in generating registrations. That will not be the case for online programs in the next stage of marketing development. We will be moving from mailing lists to e-mail lists.

The transition will be enormous and change all aspects of our marketing and promotion. E-mail will become the predominant way of communicating with past participants and best prospects. E-mail will become customized and tailored to each individual. It will become visually and graphically pleasing, with color and typesetting and pictures. E-mail will also be able to include audio messages from you, the instructor or past participants. In doing all of these things, e-mail will also impact the other aspects of our promotion and marketing, from mailed print brochures to broadcast fax to registration and more. But more important than e-mail to your program will be your e-mail lists.

Your e-mail lists will be the e-mail addresses of your past participants and your best prospects. To be on your e-mail list, two things will need to happen:

1. The person will have to want to be on your e-mail list; and
2. You will have to want the person to be on your e-mail list.

First, the person will have to want to be on your e-mail list.

There will be no junk e-mail. There can be no junk e-mail. People will not tolerate junk e-mail. Every e-mail they receive they demand it be a message they want to receive. No unwanted messages.

We are moving to an era when there will be no junk solicitations. No junk e-mail, no junk mail, no junk telemarketing.

Customers will create such negative impacts on organizations and companies that send junk e-mail that it will not be worth it for anyone to send junk e-mail. At the very least, if your message is perceived to be junk e-mail, it will not be read. The result, however, is that you can lose the customer for life. You and I won't want to risk that.

So everyone on our e-mail list will want to be on our list. That means they will want to get our messages, and they will not perceive our e-mail to be junk e-mail.

Second, you will have to want the person to be on your e-mail list.

You will not accept everyone who wants to be on your list. You will accept only those people who are likely to register in the near future, and you will have sophisticated measuring devices for evaluating whether a person is likely to register in the near future. These measuring devices are the person's past purchasing history and demographics.

Even though the cost of e-mailing unlikely prospects is low, you will have more at stake than simply promotions. You will want to form a virtual community — a select group of people. And others like them will want to join that group. And that marketing edge — having the group that others will want to join — means you will limit the group to only those people most likely to benefit from the group and from your online programs.

Your e-mail list will be a precious source of "intellectual capital," a marketing and competitive edge. You will not want to dilute that precious resource.

Your e-mail list is likely to be your past participants and those prospects who want to become new customers of your program. Your participants represent anywhere from 50 percent to 70 percent of your registrations for your next online program. So cutting down mailing and printing costs to 50 percent or more of your participants will represent a good savings to your program. You will then be able to reallocate those savings to promoting to non-customers.

The e-mail stage of promoting online courses, seminars and conferences is starting now and will become dominant sometime in the next three to five years.

You should begin building your e-mail list either:

1. Now; or
2. As soon as 50 percent of the people in your current audience have an e-mail address.

Generating E-mail Addresses

Do not look for anyone with an e-mail address. That is the wrong strategy. The right strategy is to get e-mail addresses from your best customers and current participants. You will probably get e-mail addresses from three types of people:

1. Current and past participants.
2. Prospects, those interested in attending your program.
3. Those casually interested or you have just collected the e-mail address.

These are different types of people. Code them as such, or keep them on different databases.

To get e-mail addresses of your current participants, do a survey. Develop a card that is approximately 8½" wide by 3" high, printed on card stock. On one side put a business reply address in which you are paying the postage. On the other side put a message similar to this:

Survey

We are developing additional benefits for our program participants available via e-mail. To get more information about these benefits and be on our e-mail list, please:

A. E-mail us at (your e-mail address). Include the following in the "Subject" field of your e-mail: List. Send information.
B. Or write your e-mail address below and mail this card. No postage is necessary.

___ My e-mail address is _____ .

___ I have no e-mail address.

Thank You!

Put the person's mailing label on this side of the card. Insert the card in a #10 window envelope, with the mailing label showing through the window, and mail.

You may want to consider dropping the mail-back option and only ask people to e-mail you. The reason for this is that we have found that handwritten e-mail addresses are hard to read and 50 percent of them get misread and thus are useless. You may find yourself sending a follow-up post card saying "We can't read your e-mail address." You could replace the word "write" with "type," but undoubtedly some people will hand write them. Your decision.

Begin to E-mail Now

Begin your e-mail promotions now. Gradually your e-mail promotions will generate more and more registrations. As e-mail promotions become more effective, you then redesign your direct mail promotions.

Begin now to think, plan and then generate e-mail addresses from your best participants. We will soon move from mailing lists to e-mail lists as the principal way of promoting online programs.

Promotion of the Future

A third stage in the promoting of online courses, seminars and conferences will involve a dramatically different information delivery system. These delivery systems are being pioneered and tested now. Although they are not producing lots of registrations now, they represent the way online courses will be successfully promoted in the not too distant future.

Two components in this different information delivery system are master web sites and syndication.

Master Web Sites

Master web sites are web sites listing all the online programs available. Several sites exist now. The trouble with most current master web sites is that the general public does not access them frequently and regularly.

When a master web site is promoted to the point where millions of people use it frequently and regularly, then the great panoply of online lifelong learning opportunities will unfold.

We know that there are enough people interested in just about any topic imaginable to form a course. It's just that all the people are not in the same place or on the same list. There are four people in Singapore, five in Seoul and so on. Reaching this scattered global audience for a specific topic is not feasible right now.

But if those people located your online program themselves through a master web site of all learning opportunities, then online programs could reach the general public on a global scale. Some day that will happen, hopefully within the next five to 10 years.

Syndication

A hot new information delivery system that will be developed will involve other organizations and providers. You will promote your online program through other providers.

Here's how it works. You sell "seats" or places in your online program to other providers. They will recruit participants to your program, and they will get a share of the registration fee for each person they recruit to your online course. Part of your marketing strategy will be to build a stable ongoing core of organizations to consistently promote your particular online program. Others will be doing this as well.

Part of the all-or-nothing, dominate-or-dwindle scenario of competition in the online age involves the enormous power of selling your course to other providers.

Online courses and programs that can engage the most providers will gain a huge edge over other courses in the same topic area.

Again, the online course with the best authority, lowest price and largest share going to its allied providers will win.

Chapter 15
Summary

Online learning is still in its infancy. Like the early automobile of the last century, online learning has not been perfected yet. It has many flaws. In 1903 Henry Ford's banker was reputed to have told him, "The horse and carriage is here to stay. The auto is a passing fad." Twenty years later it was too late to start an automobile company. By then all the major automobile companies that would become successful and dominate the auto industry for the rest of the century had already been formed and been doing business.

In 20 years online learning and teaching will have been tried, tested, improved and made more perfect. But today is when you want to start to teach online. Now is when the exciting future of online learning begins.

This will be the way half of all learning is delivered in this century. This is how our children and their children will learn throughout the century. And you can be among the first to help make it successful. Go do it. Be a pioneer. Teach a course online. Get out there and experiment, test and fail. It is an exciting time for learning.

Last New Year's Eve my 12-year-old son was on the computer, chatting online with his friends. He typed in a comment noting that he was looking forward to the new year. One of his chat room friends wrote back, saying that the new year was already 10 hours old and it was pretty exciting already. His chat room friend was not just in another time zone, not just in another country, but halfway around the world, where it was already the next day. Interacting with people all over the world will be normal for the next generation of learners, normal and beneficial. We are living in a new time, a time when the world needs more learning, and when your online course can be beneficial and rewarding. I wish you the best of luck with teaching online, and with learning online.

References

With online learning still in a pioneering phase, the research for this book has been necessarily oral, anecdotal and experiential. The following are people I wish to acknowledge and credit. Any inaccuracies, misinterpretations, inferences and extensions of thought belong to the author.

Chapter 1

• The reference to Kansas having mandatory continuing education on the *Wizard of Oz* is poetic license, and not true. However, the author did indeed attend a lecture on the *Wizard of Oz*.

• *Wizard of Oz* and L. Frank Baum information from a talk by a history professor Dr. Robert Luehrs, Fort Hays State University, Hays, Kansas, funded by the Kansas Humanities Council.

• Other references to Kansas history in the late nineteenth century are from exhibits at the Kansas Historical Museum, Topeka, Kansas.

Chapter 2

• The Gerald Celente quote is from his book, *Trends 2000,* Warner Books, New York, NY, 1997, page 249.

• Washington Post references from *Teaching Online,* by Debbie Goldberg, *Washington Post* web site, April 5, 1998.

• For background information on the plow and tractor, I am indebted to Professor Andrew Barkley, Department of Agricultural Economics, Kansas State University, Manhattan, Kansas.

• Reference to the military and cavalry from *FDR: Into the Storm,* by Kenneth S. Davis, 1993.

- Reference to one-room school houses in the State of Washington from *Encyclopedia Britannica*, Volume 23, page 389, University of Chicago, Chicago, Illinois, 1945.
- Peter J. Denning's quote from his manuscript, *How We Will Learn,* October 1996, George Mason University, Fairfax, Virginia, page 2.
- Reference to Keio University from "Japan Shuts Down Its Education Assembly Line," by Gale Eisenstodt, *Fast Company Magazine,* February/March 1997, pages 40-42.
- For more on self-directed learning and adult education, see Malcolm Knowles *The Adult Learner: A Neglected Species,* 1973, Gulf Publishing, Houston, page 42.
- Several Internet references are owed to Richard Thieme, consultant and futurist, Fox Point, Wisconsin, from a speech at the Metcom conference, April 4, 1996, in Chicago.
- University Online Publishing reference to online courses from Dees Stallings, University Online Publishing, Fairfax, Virginia.
- Distance and online learning data from Paula Peinovich, Regents College, Albany, NY.
- For the seminal and best work on virtual community, see *Net Gain* by John Hagel and Arthur G. Armstrong, Harvard Business School Press, Boston, 1997. Another excellent related work is *Cybercorp,* by James Martin, Amacom Books, New York, NY, 1996.
- *Positioning* is a classic marketing book by Al Ries and Jack Trout, 1981, first edition.

Chapter 3

- *History of Frankfort, Kansas,* from the Frankfort, Kansas, Library, June Warren, librarian.

Chapter 5

- The best book on integrative learning and in-person teaching in the 21st century is *Mastering the Teaching of Adults* by Jerold Apps, 1991, Krieger Publishing, Melbourne, Florida.

Chapter 6

• See J. Roby Kidd's *How Adults Learn,* Association Press, New York, 1973, 1959.

Chapter 7

• *The One to One Future* is by Don Peppers and Martha Rogers, Doubleday, New York, NY 1993.

Chapter 8

• Background information on e-mail from Leonard Charnoff, Internet and e-mail guru, Gaston, Oregon.

Chapter 13

• Russell Robinson's work is from *Helping Adults Learn and Change,* Omnibook Company, Milwaukee, Wisconsin, 1979, page 50.

• Philip C. Candy's work is from *Self-Direction for Lifelong Learning,* Jossey-Bass Publishers, San Francisco, CA, 1991, page 391.

• Florence Nelson's work is from *Yes, You Can Teach,* Carma Press, St. Paul, MN, 1977, page 4.

Chapter 14

• With regard to the concept of syndication of online courses, I am indebted to Dorothy Durkin, New York University, New York.

More Resources on Teaching Online

LERN is regularly developing new information regarding online learning, teaching online, and developing and marketing online courses. For the latest information about articles, seminars, web site services, online seminars, newsletters, training and consulting, contact the Learning Resources Network (LERN).

E-mail: info@lern.org

URL: www.lern.org

Phone: 1-800-678-5376 (US and Canada)

Fax: 1-888-234-8633 (worldwide)

Write: LERN, PO Box 9, River Falls, WI 54022.

About LERN

The Learning Resources Network (LERN) is the leading association in lifelong learning programming, offering information and consulting expertise to providers of lifelong learning programs.

Begun in 1974, LERN serves more than 9,000 professionals every year by providing practical, how-to information on marketing, finances, management, and product development. It is information not available anywhere else.

Services include publications; newsletters; seminars, conferences, Institutes and in-house training programs; and consulting to members and others. LERN's Internet Information Services include more than 450 reports on the management and marketing of continuing education programming; online discussions with colleagues from around the world; news; surveys, and more.

LERN serves a wide variety of institutions, including state universities, four-year colleges, colleges within universities, private colleges, community colleges, technical colleges, public schools, recreation departments, and associations.

Every year we research and disseminate the most advanced and sophisticated information. Recent work has included: profit margins—what makes money; redesigning of job descriptions; the information specialist position; an action strategy for internal marketing; developing a product mix for your segments; why you need seven market segments; the shift from products to markets; and how to measure staff time.

LERN is a nonprofit, tax-exempt, educational organization. We are led by a Board of Directors, with daily operations carried out by 20 staff and consultants located in three offices around the country.

LERN's mission is to extend lifelong learning to all. Our vision statement is: "to be the authoritative, distinctive source of practical information related to lifelong learning programs." Our slogan is *"Information That Works!"®*

Bulk Discounts

Order for everyone in your organization!

Up to 50% off. Discount prices.

1-9 copies, $14.95 each
10-24 copies, $9.95 each
25 or more copies, $7.45 each (50% off)
For 100 or more copies, contact LERN.

_____
Name

_____
Title or Department (if any)

_____
Organization

_____
Address

_____
City, State/Province, Zip/Postal Code

_____
E-mail Address

_____
Phone

Please send me _____(quantity) copies of *Teaching Online* by William A. Draves at _____ (price per copy), or $ _____ subtotal.

Shipping $_____
Total $_____
Shipping and Handling:

Please check one:
____Credit Card
____Bill me, purchase order enclosed

To Order
Call: 1-800-678-5376 (US and Canada)
Fax toll free: 1-888-234-8633 (worldwide)
Email: info@lern.org
Web site orders: http://www.lern.org
Mail to: LERN Books, PO Box 9, River Falls, WI 54022 U.S.A.